I0820208

Draw Close to Jesus

Draw Close to Jesus

40 Encounters *with the* **Savior** *for the* **Sacred Season** *of* **Lent**

Heidi Chiavaroli

Revell
a division of Baker Publishing Group
Grand Rapids, Michigan

Published by Revell
a division of Baker Publishing Group
Grand Rapids, Michigan
RevellBooks.com

Printed in China

Library of Congress Cataloging-in-Publication Data
Names: Chiavaroli, Heidi, author
Title: Draw close to Jesus : 40 encounters with the Savior for the sacred season of Lent / Heidi Chiavaroli.
Description: Grand Rapids, Michigan : Revell, a division of Baker Publishing Group, [2026]
Identifiers: LCCN 2025020744 | ISBN 9780800746544 cloth | ISBN 9781493452668 ebook
Subjects: LCSH: Jesus Christ—Meditations | Bible. Gospels—Devotional literature | Lent—Prayers and devotions | LCGFT: Devotional literature. | Prayers. | Meditations.
Classification: LCC BV85 .C478 2026 | DDC 242/.34—dc23/eng/20250711
LC record available at https://lccn.loc.gov/2025020744

Cover design by Laura Klynstra

Published in association with Books & Such Literary Management, www.booksandsuch.com.

Baker Publishing Group publications use paper produced from sustainable forestry practices and postconsumer waste whenever possible.

26 27 28 29 30 31 32 7 6 5 4 3 2 1

To Sarah and Mike Pudlo and my brothers
and sisters at Journey Christian Church.
Thank you for helping to challenge
and grow my faith in and love for Jesus.

Contents

Glossary

abba—Father

Adonai—Lord

bet ha-midrash—"House of study," higher learning to study the Torah

bet sefer—"House of the book," synagogue school

calamus—Writing reed

gabbai—Collector of taxes

haphtarah—Selection from one of the books of the Prophets read in synagogue after the reading of the Torah

HaShem— "The name," as in the name of God; often spoken in place of YHWH, the name revealed to Moses in Exodus, which was considered too holy to be uttered

hazzan—Guardian of the sacred books and minister of the synagogue

huppah—Wedding canopy

ima—Mother

ketubah—Marriage contract

mezuzah—Small parchment scroll upon which the words of the Shema are written

Migdal Eder—"Tower of the Flock," a watchtower located on the road between Bethlehem and Jerusalem

prutah—Small coin, equivalent to a thousandth of a pound

rabboni—Teacher

Ruach Hako'desh—The Holy Spirit

Shabbat—Sabbath

shalom—"Peace," a greeting or farewell

Shavuot—"Festival of Weeks," commemoration of Moses receiving the law on Mount Sinai

Shekinah—The divine presence of God

Shevat—Winter months

shiva—Weeklong period of mourning

shofar—Ram's horn

tali—Historic Roman version of knucklebones

tefillin—Small black leather boxes containing scrolls of parchment inscribed with verses from the Torah, worn during weekday morning prayers

terni lapilli—Early variation of tic-tac-toe

Trisagion—Three times holy

tzitzit—Prayer tassels

yahrzeit—The anniversary of a death

Yerushalayim—Jerusalem

Introduction

Encountering Jesus Through Imaginative Remembering

I will never forget the year I walked away from the church. After a flourishing relationship with Christ and an impressive résumé of service to my local church, I woke up one day, nearly fifteen years into the journey, to realize with fearful clarity that I'd lost something along the way. Something quite important.

I was incredibly fearful I had lost Jesus himself.

I wasn't serving God. I was doing what I thought was expected of me. I was serving in order to get outcomes. I'd stopped spending time in the Scriptures. Prayer was an afterthought. I dreaded going to church.

I'd gotten so caught up in doing things *for* Jesus, I neglected to spend time *with* Jesus.

I'd like to tell you I recognized the problem right away and turned to God to set my motivations straight. But that was not the case. This was a long, painful journey where I groped around in the dark with my doubts for what had once been mine—*the joy of knowing Jesus.*

During that time, the thought of church created an anxiety so thorough I couldn't bear to go back. Like a spoon-fed toddler, I could only handle small bits of Scripture. Too often, I equated God and his Word to the hurt I'd experienced and to the stress I'd placed on myself surrounding my church duties.

One small passage that came to me during this time, however, was enough to keep my hope alive. Beautiful, grace-drenched words from Jesus in Matthew 11:28–30: "Come to me all you who are weary and burdened, and I will give you rest. Take my yoke upon you and learn from me, for I am gentle and humble in heart, and you will find rest for your souls. For my yoke is easy and my burden is light."

Come to me.

I am gentle and humble.

I will give you rest.

This is not what I had been living. Then again, I hadn't been tarrying with Jesus—I'd been seeking the approval of religious culture. But this invitation to rest in my Savior? *I wanted that.*

It just so happened that this new calling found me in the season of Lent. And with immense gratitude, I stoked to life the embers of a sacred season laid dormant with my childhood. I embraced the slowing down. The liturgy. The church calendar. Repentance. Fasting. Measures of charity and justice. The unhurried intentionality of it all. I hungered for the timeless truths and practices of the Christian faith, and I savored that hunger. I stumbled into a sea of grace contained within the magnificent rhythms of the church year—rhythms that reminded me of the gospel story. Rhythms that reminded me of God's immeasurable grace. Birth to life, death to resurrection.

Lent was about finding the breath of the Spirit and losing myself, repenting not just in a onetime Sinner's prayer, but repenting as a rule of life so that Jesus might sweep in and renew my spirit with the grace of true spiritual rest that leads to restoration again and again, every minute of every day.

As I reread the four Gospels with fresh eyes, I found a renewed appreciation for this Jesus who attracted the tired, the poor, the outcast, the tax collector, the leper, the stubborn fisherman, the staunch zealot, the uncertain Pharisee.

Through the Gospel stories, God pushed back the curtain of church hurt and gave me fresh hope. He restored my faith. He did not abandon me in that desperate place.

As I read, I remembered why I'd come to Jesus in the first place all those years ago. I remembered my own spiritual poverty. Away from the product that had become my Christianity, I saw who Jesus was. And I wanted nothing more than to walk with him.

I thought of the many accounts of needy humanity meeting Jesus, and even of the accounts that were not written (see John 20:30). I thought of a child who comes to him but is brushed aside by a well-meaning disciple. A Roman centurion who drives the nails into Jesus's hands and yet, miraculously, is granted forgiveness. A Bethlehem woman who receives an unexpected guest on the thirtieth anniversary of her babe's death at the hands of Herod's soldiers.

Each person had an entire story I could only imagine. And imagine I did.

I am a writer, after all. Imagination comes with the territory. What better use for it than to place myself in the skin of those whose lives Jesus touched? Those who were drawn to this carpenter from Nazareth who upset political expectations, performed audacious miracles and healings, and ultimately claimed to be the Son of God?

To my delight, I discovered these imaginative exercises were not as uncommon as I initially assumed. From Brother Lawrence (1611–91) to St. Ignatius of Loyola (1491–1556), I discovered holy practices fueled by the imagination.

What's more, it seems it might not be far off from what the original authors of the Bible were trying to convey. In the foreword to the New American Standard Bible, the translators say that "Greek authors frequently used the present tense for the sake of heightened vividness, thereby transporting their readers in imagination to the actual scene at the time of occurrence" (The Lockman Foundation, 2020).

I love what these Greek authors were trying to do! They were placing their readers in the story by the choice of their words. In a culture that valued retelling their history in the stories of their heritage, they were asking their readers to imagine and remember. To *remember* what they came from in order to be restored to the Lord, to be refreshed.

After rescuing the Israelites from slavery in Egypt, the Lord told them to *remember* what he had done for them. To play it out, again and again. To imagine it in their minds' eyes. Even Jesus, during the Last Supper, instructed his disciples to break bread together, saying, "Do this in remembrance of me" (Luke 22:19).

Remember. Don't forget. Run the script over and over again so that it becomes a part of you, until the power and experience of that memory writes itself into the present, where you live today. Until it writes itself into your heart, mind, soul, and very being.

In a contemporary world where our screens are constantly imagining for us, there's value in remembering Jesus through the power of our own imaginations. There's value in meditating and savoring the biblical stories in order to behold his beauty. In slipping into the shoes (or more accurately, sandals!) of those who walked with Jesus on earth, we are able to enter the story ourselves. In doing this, I am thoroughly convinced we will draw closer to him.

The season of Lent helped me recover the intended beauty of the liturgy and of the church. This is a season for repenting. But it's also a season for remembering. For aligning ourselves with the workings of the Lord. For coming to the one who stepped into our sin, our inadequacies, and our shortcomings. For remembering and then anticipating because we know the amazing splendor of the empty grave is upon us. Death is defeated. Grace sweeps in.

In this book, you will find forty imaginative retellings—one meant to be read for each day of Lent. While these stories are based on Scripture and historical research, they are fictional narratives *based* on biblical accounts. I pray these retellings draw you deeper into the Gospel stories but would not replace your time in God's Word. I pray they stir you to marinate *in* the Scriptures, to answer Jesus's call when he says, "Come to me."

May God's glory abound in your life, my sibling in Christ, and may this season of Lent find you resting—and remembering—in him.

With hope,
Heidi

ONE

The Virgin's Secret

Inspired by Matthew 1 and Luke 1:26–56

Mary bids farewell to the family she has traveled with from Ein Karem, her middle trembling like the threads on her cousin Elizabeth's loom. Already, she misses her older kinswoman—the bond she found with her, the wisdom she offered . . . the acceptance.

Will she find any of that here in Nazareth?

She bites her lip, thinking of Joseph. Perhaps she should have told him of the angel's visit before she left for Zechariah and Elizabeth's home. But she'd been filled with doubts. She hadn't even told her mother. Only Salome knows her secret.

A secret everyone in Nazareth would soon know.

She walks down the dirt road with bone-weary limbs, the flowered hills and purple haze of Mount Carmel doing nothing to ease the tension in her chest. Shouldering her leather bag with the precious gift of the swaddling cloths Zechariah gave her, Mary walks past the empty flat-roofed synagogue.

She remembers Elizabeth's beautiful words—words that cast aside her doubts and sealed the truth of all she'd experienced within her heart.

Blessed is she who has believed that the Lord would fulfill his promises to her!

"Mary!"

Her sister runs toward her, the dust from the road puffing up the hem of the younger woman's tunic, her headscarf flying behind her. When Salome's arms come around her, Mary sinks into them. She inhales the scents of hay and lemons and fresh-baked bread.

All too soon, Salome pulls back. Her eyes widen at Mary's stomach. No robe can hide her secret any longer.

"You . . . you are . . ." For the first time, Mary's younger sister appears at a loss for words. "The angel. He spoke truth?"

Mary presses her lips together, wonder and dread swirling through her in a thunderous tumult. "Elizabeth is also pregnant."

A smile brightens Salome's face. "Just as Gabriel proclaimed!"

"Our cousin knew I was with child before I told her."

Salome pulls Mary toward their home. "Have you seen Joseph?"

"No."

Mary follows Salome up the street where lines of sand-colored houses embrace terraced gardens and soft palms. Twisted fig trees and graceful olives stand in the background, an entrance to fertile pastureland brimming with flax flowers alongside pale gold fields of barley.

They climb the stairs to Mary's childhood home, a stone and mud structure cut into the rocky hillside. She raises her fingers to the mezuzah fixed to the doorpost before bringing them to her lips. The warmth of the fire greets her. Her mother stands at the kiln, taking out a loaf of barley bread. When she sees Mary, she nearly drops the loaf into the hot coals.

"Child!" She rushes to embrace her. Mary closes her eyes, the child moving within as if sensing the presence of his grandmother. A longing for Mary's father fills her. She thinks of his body resting in their family's grave with their ancestors. The last act of his life was securing a ketubah with Joseph ben Jacob for his oldest daughter.

Her mother gasps and pulls back, her face pale in the firelight. Her gaze drops to her oldest daughter's middle. "Mary." She gropes for a chair. "How can this be? Did Joseph . . ."

Mary falls to the beaten earth at her mother's feet. "No, Ima. Joseph has not laid a hand upon me."

"Who, then, child? A soldier? A rebel on the road to Ein Karem? I knew I should not have agreed to you leaving us! We are ruined." She breaks into sobs.

"Ima, please listen to me." Mary grasps her mother's wrinkled hands, calloused from turning the millstones to grind barley grain into flour. "Before I left to see Elizabeth, I was visited by the angel Gabriel."

"Mary." Shame fringes the older woman's voice.

"He told me I was to bear a child. That the Ruach Hako'desh would come upon me, and I would bear the Son of the Most High."

Her mother looks as if she will tear her tunic. Mary rushes on. "He said Elizabeth was with child as well, and Ima, she is! I speak the truth."

Salome drops to the floor alongside Mary. "She does, Ima. Mary told me before she left. It must be true, for Elizabeth is pregnant, even in her old years!"

Their mother shakes her head. "I do not see. I do not see how this could be at all. Your abba would be disgraced. Joseph . . . he is a righteous man. He will not stand for this. Mary, you could be stoned." Her last word begins a desperate wail.

"I speak the truth," Mary says again.

"Mary?"

She stands at the sound of the familiar voice. Joseph.

He is ordinary in height and looks, and yet she has grown fond of him since their betrothal. He helped their small family when her father died, even sneaking their goat extra grain from his pockets when no one was looking. She has missed the sight of him, how his dark hair curls at his neck, how his eyes lighten when he bids her shalom on her way to the well.

Now, his hair and beard are freshly combed and oiled. No doubt he has wondered over her absence.

His eyes fall to her stomach. Disbelief carves his features. His crestfallen expression pierces her heart.

He bunches his fists at his side, his face red as ocher. "Mary?"

She longs to go to him, to assure him she has not been unfaithful. Instead, she stays put.

Her touch will not be welcome.

"I am so sorry, Joseph." Mary's mother does not say they cannot repay the money he gave upon the signing of the ketubah. He knows.

Joseph bites his lip, looks wildly around the room. Mary does not mistake the wetness in his eyes. He does not care about the money he will lose.

He loves her.

The realization makes all this more difficult.

Adonai, how will I raise the Son of the Most High on my own? Why should this good man be wounded by this child?

Joseph sets his jaw, avoiding Mary. "I will divorce her quietly."

Her mother's fingers flutter to her throat. "Thank you. Thank you, Joseph, for your mercy."

He raises wounded eyes to Mary.

"You are a righteous man. Thank you, Joseph," Mary says before he turns and rushes from her home.

That night, tears course onto the stone pillow beneath Mary's head. She longs for Elizabeth. She longs for the light in Joseph's eyes she will never know again. Yes, she is sure of HaShem's provision, but a terrible dread comes upon her that although the angel proclaimed she was blessed among women, that blessing does not preclude the immanent pain that comes with this responsibility.

She is alone. Her friends will want nothing to do with her. Her firstborn will have no father to recognize his legitimacy after he has been washed and rubbed with salt. She will never know what it is like to lie next to Joseph as his wife. To have a home of her own. To be loved by a man.

She wonders if she will be subjected to the trial of bitter water laid out in Torah.

Adonai, give me strength to be your servant to the end.

She remembers Elizabeth's words. She remembers the song tucked close to her heart.

My soul magnifies the Lord, and my spirit rejoices in God my Savior, because he has looked with favor on the lowly state of his servant . . .

Salome wraps her arms around her, her sister's warm body a comfort in the darkness. Adonai *has* provided her with at least one person who believes her. For that, she is grateful.

"We will pray, yes?" Salome whispers.

Mary falls asleep to Salome's prayer, one they long ago memorized from the scroll of the prophet Isaiah. Her sleep is deep, and she does not wake until sunlight shines in her room and a knock sounds at the door.

She rubs her back as she walks through the empty house to open the door.

Joseph stands at the threshold.

She stumbles back. Has he changed his mind? Will he drag her to the town square to be stoned before the synagogue?

But he does not look angry. His eyes are bright. The light she never thought to know again—the light of his favor—is alive in his gaze. He practically bounces on his heels.

"Mary."

"Joseph?"

He grasps her hands, and she sinks into the warm calluses of his skin, into the security and acceptance his touch provides.

"He will be called Jesus, because he will save his people from their sins."

Reflection Questions

Read Mary's song in Luke 1:46–55. What reflection of Jesus do you see in his mother's words? Use your imagination to picture the role she is to play in his upbringing.

Joseph went above the law to claim a nobler form of justice in not divorcing Mary. When might religious expectations restrict us from loving how God loves?

Prayer

Heavenly Father, thank you for Mary's and Joseph's obedience to your calling. Grant us eyes and hearts for the outcast among us, that we might extend your love to the downtrodden and ashamed. Help us see our own spiritual poverty as we look with fresh eyes to those around us. Amen.

Suggested Reading

Matthew 1

Luke 1:26–56

TWO

The Shepherd's Tale

Inspired by Luke 2:8–20

He eases the lamb from its mother's womb, uttering words of encouragement to the ewe that has labored for the better part of the night to push her offspring into the world.

"There you are, Ima. Your babe is almost here."

He lays the swaddling cloths on the ground. The lamb slides forth in a bloom of liquid white.

A male. He is beautiful, perfection.

The ewe stands to clean off her firstborn and Rani watches the tender exchange, his chest lurching at the knowledge that this perfect lamb will not grow to adulthood. Like all the animals surrounding Yerushalayim, this one too will be consecrated to HaShem. And, being a male, he will make a suitable offering on the altar during Passover.

He takes the lamb in his arms and tucks the swaddling cloths around it. The fabric will keep the babe warm and its tender skin safe from bruising, preserving the small animal as a worthy temple sacrifice.

He tries not to think of the lamb's soft throat being slit by a temple priest on its eighth day of life, of its body being burned on the altar in the Court of the Priests. He once made the mistake of speaking such thoughts to Father.

"If you do not wish to watch a lamb perish on your behalf, then do not sin." His father had said the words with a sarcastic sneer.

Do not sin.

While every ancestor of Abraham and Jacob knows this to be impossible, he and his father know Rani to be especially hopeless in this area. It's a pity the older man never lets his oldest son—his only son—forget it.

Rani looks off toward the watchtower of Migdal Eder, the burial place of Jacob's beloved wife Rachel. Rani himself is a descendant of Levi ben Jacob, and his family has taken on the mantle of Levitical shepherds for centuries.

The lamb squirms in his arms and he remembers the first time he'd helped birth a lamb. The first time he'd wrapped a precious, pure animal in swaddling cloths. That day, his eight-year-old brother, Benesh, had begged to join him. Although Rani had agreed, he resented Benesh's company. At eleven, Rani wanted to prove to their father he could tend the flock by himself.

But all that was forgotten when the ewe had brought forth a spotless lamb. In truth, Rani had done little to help, but the lamb was born on his watch, and so he could lay claim to it.

After the allotted seven days with its mother, he gathered the lamb in fresh swaddling cloths. Though Benesh despised being alone in the fields, Rani handed him his rod and staff, instructing his brother to stay with the sheep, to keep them together and protect them from wild beasts. He had not waited for Benesh's agreement before rushing toward the city to find his father.

The older man would be pleased to see the spotless young lamb, to know he could trust his oldest son with such an important task. At the city gates, Rani heard Benesh calling after him. He silently cursed his brother for leaving the sheep. As always, though, his brother followed him. Rani ran faster through the sloping cobbled streets, the lamb still cradled in his arms. Benesh called again, but Rani ignored him. It would be just like his younger brother to claim recognition for the lamb's birth. As the last child their mother bore before her death, Benesh could commit no wrong in Father's sight.

When Rani ducked around the chariot of the imperial family to escape Benesh, he had not expected his small brother to follow. To get caught beneath the heavy wheels.

He had not expected the sacrifice for his pride to be the death of his little brother. A brother who wanted nothing more than his presence.

Now, Rani swallows back emotion. He has offered many sacrifices the past six years for his sin, but the guilt remains. Father ensures it, as does his own heart.

Will he forever provide animal sacrifices for other people's forgiveness, but never find forgiveness for himself?

A great flash lights the sky, and the newborn lamb, warm in his arms, quivers. Rani waits for a chorus of thunder, but none comes. The light brightens the blue-black heavens, obliterating the moon and the stars with its brilliance, blanketing the fields and the Migdal Eder in a light purer than the sun's.

Rani's limbs tremble. The ewes bleat and stomp their hooves. Will all of Judah end in this moment?

And then there is the blast of a threefold trumpet, reminiscent of the Trisagion that sounds when a sacrifice is laid upon the altar. Heaven and earth meld into one, and a man in a robe whiter than that of a temple priest's descends upon the fields, enveloping Rani's flock and his cousins in what can only be the glory of the Shekinah.

Rani stands on quivering legs, his rod and staff forgotten on the ground, nothing but the lamb in his arms.

The angel speaks.

"Do not be afraid. I bring you good news that will cause great joy for all the people."

The words solidify in Rani's mind like dew appearing on night grass. How can this be?

"Today in the town of David a Savior has been born to you; he is the Messiah, the Lord. This will be a sign to you: You will find a baby wrapped in cloths and lying in a manger."

The Messiah? The Messiah born this night? A Savior wrapped in humble swaddling cloths, just like the lamb in his arms?

The sky lights with a host of angels so large they number the stars. The most beautiful music sounds around Rani, drawing forth an ache of longing in his chest.

"Glory to God in the highest heaven, and on earth peace to those on whom his favor rests."

And then they are gone, nothing but their words lingering in the cool of the starry night air.

Peace to those on whom his favor rests.

That the angels would bring this message to a dreadful sinner like himself overwhelms him. He sinks to the ground, the lamb tucked beneath his arm.

"Cousin!" Abel runs toward him, waving his staff. "HaShem has blessed us. Let us go and see that which the angels spoke of."

Another of his cousins hurries to them. "My helper will watch our flocks until we return from Bethlehem."

Yes, of course. Bethlehem. The scroll of Micah told of the Savior to be born in the city, but never had Rani thought to see it with his own eyes. He stumbles south with the other shepherds.

The moon rises higher as they make their way to the small city. Most of the homes are dark, but one shines with light, and they rush toward it. A woman with a bucket of water opens the door, stopping short at the sight of them.

Abel trips over his words about the angels, begs the woman to let them inside to worship the Messiah.

When she agrees, they spill into the humble home. The main room holds a donkey and there, in the feeding trough by his parents, is a babe wrapped in swaddling cloths identical to those that wrap the lamb in Rani's arms.

Rani falls to his knees, tears pricking his eyes at the sight of the perfect babe in such a humble state. The Messiah. A Savior for his people.

He looks down at the beautiful white lamb still snug in his arms.

All he knows is what the swaddling cloths represent. All he knows is the angel's words.

I bring you good news that will cause great joy for all the people.

He bows low, the depth of his need causing a well of gratitude to burst within him.

HaShem has made a way not only for his people but, it seems, for Rani as well.

Reflection Questions

Read 1 John 1:5–2:2. What does John say about sin?

These Levitical shepherds likely knew their Old Testament well. They knew the Messiah would be born near their home, and yet when the angels found them, they were doing their ordinary work. How can you honor God through your ordinary work?

Prayer

God Almighty, sometimes we don't fully comprehend the gravity of our sin and sometimes we feel buried beneath its weight. Help us find the delicate balance between acknowledging our iniquity and knowing our worth in your eyes. Thank you for the life and freedom we find in Jesus. Amen.

Suggested Reading

Luke 2:8–20

THREE

The Waiting Prophetess

Inspired by Luke 2:25–40

Anna shuffles through the Court of the Gentiles, past the money changers and the lambs and doves being sold for sacrifices. The strident voices of the doctors of the law arguing with one another mix with the sound of clinking coins. The temple hums with the bustle of activity and conversation, the bleating of lambs a constant background noise.

Intent on her purpose, Anna climbs the steps of the Beautiful Gate and slips into the reverent folds of the inner temple.

In the Court of Women, men, women, and children mill about, turning in their sacrificial animals to the priests and dropping their offerings into the trumpet-shaped chests by the doors. As always, she looks straight to the Corinthian bronze of the Nicanor Gate. Its fifteen steps lead to the Court of Israel where the men worship, their prayers mingling with the fragrant incense from the Golden Altar, their eyes getting the best view of the barefooted priests and the sacrificial offerings.

She hobbles up the two small steps of the raised dais where the women worship. Through the Nicanor Gate, she sees the great open cedar door of the sanctuary, which reveals a glimpse of the magnificent, embroidered curtain hiding the Holy Place. Each court inches closer and closer to the most sacred dwelling place of HaShem—the Holy of Holies.

A place she, as a woman, will never get any closer to than this. Unless . . .

She thinks of the Levitical shepherds rushing into the temple last month, their faces aglow, their words remarkable. News of a host of angels. News of a baby born in Bethlehem.

Her heart had stuttered with anticipation at their words. And since then, she has prayed in hopeful expectation, even as she realizes an ossuary will likely hide her bones by the time a baby Messiah ushers in HaShem's kingdom.

And yet, if she has honored Adonai in her prayers and fasting over the years, perhaps it will be enough. It is *more* than enough that her ancient ears heard the shepherds' hope.

If only Akivah had lived to see the building of the temple. Her husband of seven years had often frequented their synagogue and mourned for a place where their people could worship together. He would certainly rejoice to see her now.

Rejoice? She bites back a sad smile, thinking of her husband's handsome young face on the morning of their wedding, of the strong voice of her bridegroom calling for her outside her family's home.

If Akivah saw her now, he would not recognize her ancient skin, her withered curves. Eighty-four years have plucked away at her youthful beauty, once a mark of the women of her tribe. Now, her bones throb with age.

After the loss of her husband, Anna had soaked herself in deep mourning—grief not only over Akivah but over her barren womb as well. She committed the rest of her years to Adonai, fasting, praying, and never leaving the temple after it was built.

Atop the platform, Anna kneels on tile, her creaking limbs protesting. As soon as she settles, however, her calloused knees conform to the long-held position and she sinks into it, her body anticipating what the posture means for her soul.

The priests sprinkle the altar with blood, pouring out the lifeblood of the young animals at the base of the slab. After the sacrifices are finished, the priests bless those in the temple with a benediction. The Levites play instruments on the steps of the Nicanor Gate, the glorious sound of the Trisagion filling the temple.

Anna's heart settles into the familiar words, into the community of her people mingling in the presence of Adonai. Joy flows through her veins.

Holy God, Holy and Mighty, Holy Immortal, have mercy upon us.

After the service, the temple empties. Only those who bought special services or who linger in prayer remain.

Quiet is left in the wake of the diminishing crowd. Gone is any pretense or show. Peace remains.

Anna prostrates herself before HaShem.

Shema Yisrael: Adonai Eloheinu, Adonai Echad!

Hear, O Israel: the Lord your God, the Lord is One!

She finishes the Shema when a shout of praise draws her attention toward the steps of the Nicanor Gate. Simeon. The faithful old man is usually demure and silent. What caused such an outburst?

Simeon holds his arms out to a man and woman in simple garb who stand before him. The woman hands him a bundle wrapped in cloths.

Anna's skin prickles. A baby. A redemption ceremony, then—a way to remember Adonai paving a way for the Hebrew firstborn sons in Egypt during the tenth plague. Normally a solemn affair.

Only . . . it has been just over forty days since the shepherds told of the angels appearing. The exact time for a babe's purification rites at the temple.

She scrambles to her feet, stumbling and catching herself.

A baby. The baby of whom the shepherds spoke?

She eases off the steps of the platform, straining to hear Simeon's words as she pushes her trembling legs toward the young couple.

"Sovereign Lord, as you have promised, you may now dismiss your servant in peace. For my eyes have seen your salvation, which you have prepared in the sight of all nations: a light for revelation to the Gentiles, and the glory of your people Israel."

Any doubts as to the child's identity vanish at the bold cadence of Simeon's voice echoing the scroll of Isaiah. And when her gaze falls on the tiny babe in his ancient, gnarled hands, the whispering wind of the Holy Spirit brushes hope and joy across her weary heart.

Anna stands next to the parents, who stare with wide eyes at Simeon with the babe. The old man raises his hand and blesses first the father, and then the mother. But his hand hovers over the young woman's head. "This child is destined to cause the falling and rising of many in Israel, and to be a sign that will be spoken against, so that the thoughts of many hearts will be revealed." His kind, dark eyes sober. "And a sword will pierce your own soul too."

Anna breathes deep. A Nunc Dimittis. A beautiful promise that comes with a warning. What could it mean?

Simeon places the babe back into the arms of his mother. Her youthful face is pale and somber beneath the light of the lampstand.

Anna places a hand of comfort on the woman's arm and then touches the infant's swaddled legs. The warmth of the babe seeps into her knotted fingers.

Words of praise bubble up in Anna's throat. "Praise HaShem for the redemption of his people and for this good news, the consolation of Israel. Praise him for revealing himself to the humble and lowly and for meeting our longing with the promise of our redemption."

A tear rolls down the mother's cheek. "Thank you," she whispers to Simeon and Anna. "I know the beginning, and I suppose now I know something of the end." She glances at Simeon, who speaks to the father.

Anna squeezes her arm. "Only Adonai knows the end, dear one. Your heart may be pierced, but even in this, HaShem is faithful. Trust in one who has known pain in her lifetime."

She brushes her tears away and nods. "I am grateful."

"Please, what is his name?" Anna chokes out the words as her gaze again falls to the sleeping child.

"Jesus."

The Lord is my salvation.

Of course.

It is suddenly unimportant that she can never move past the Nicanor Gate. For today, with this news and with the warmth from the babe still coursing through her fingers, her soul is satisfied.

She knows his presence, for she has seen the face of her Lord.

Reflection Questions

Lent is a time of fasting, prayer, repentance, and preparation. How does Anna's example inspire you in this season?

Read Luke 2:34. Meditate on Mary and Joseph raising the child Jesus while knowing a glimpse of what is ahead.

Prayer

Holy Father, to think of you coming as a vulnerable babe for all people—those who feel they belong and those who don't, those who seek you out and those you surprise with your grace—fills us with gratitude. May the knowledge of your presence and the light of your salvation reveal our hearts to us even as you refine them. Thank you for your word and for this truth you've bestowed upon us. Amen.

Suggested Reading

Luke 2:25–40

FOUR

A Father's Heart

Inspired by Luke 2:41–52

He does not understand how such a thing could happen. He does not understand how he could have *allowed* it to happen.

Joseph glances at his wife, who worries her bottom lip between her teeth. "We will find him, Mary. Do not fear." He nods, as if to seal his promise, as if to urge his words to life.

They will find him.

In all his twelve years, Jesus has never given him or his mother any trouble. Was he to begin now, on the cusp of manhood?

Not until they were a day's journey from Yerushalayim on their way home to Nazareth from their Passover celebration had they realized their son was missing from their caravan. How had Jesus missed their departure? He always did what was expected of him, always paid careful attention to the comings and goings and needs of his family.

Which explained the worry lines on Mary's face. Jesus would never willingly disobey them, which meant perhaps he was in harm's way.

At the thought, Joseph picks up his pace. Mary does not protest. This time, their trip to the Holy City is nothing like the first, with their merry caravan from Nazareth anticipating the journey and the Paschal Feast. Laughing. Reminiscing. Chanting the Psalms of Ascent.

The older children had followed in the back, frolicking with cousins and siblings and friends, enjoying a break from Torah school and the work of the fields, anticipating the sights and sounds of Yerushalayim.

Now, the dazzling temple mount rises in view for the second time in six days. Its crown of white marble and shimmering gold rises high over yawning valleys. The Roman fortress melds with the ocher houses and the white roof of the palace, all surrounding the temple in their protection. This time, there is no cheerful band. Joseph and Mary's other children are in the care of her sister's family.

Joseph remembers stopping in this very place several days earlier. Jesus had joined them as they neared the grand city, and Joseph placed a hand on his oldest son's shoulder. This moment never failed to elicit complicated emotions within him. Admiration. Pride. Wonder.

But curiously, he had not seen any of those emotions on Jesus's face. In fact, Joseph could not name what was etched on the boy's features. Longing? Sadness?

Whatever it was disappeared as they entered the city, the press of people in the marketplace and temple courts too distracting for deep thoughts and ponderings. They'd offered the festive sacrifice in the temple, as well as their Omer offerings of barley for the priests to wave before HaShem. They'd eaten the Passover Seder with Zachariah's cousin Eyal ben Abel.

"He was quiet since we arrived." Mary's breaths are labored as they climb a steep valley.

Joseph cannot deny it. Ever since Jesus first gazed at the temple, ever since he witnessed the offering of the sacrificial lamb on the temple altar . . .

"We will find him," he repeats, their steps more urgent as they pass through the gates of the city. On the twisting maze of cobbled streets, they climb stairs while seeking the one they lost, the one they love.

Joseph tries not to think of the first time he held Jesus in his arms and placed him in that manger. Of the fierce protection he felt over mother and child as they fled to Egypt. And then, the blessed return to Nazareth. Teaching Jesus to shape stone and wood, teaching him Torah and the wonders of Adonai.

He recalls his son's voice as a child, standing at the workbench, stone hammer in hand, reciting the sacrificial ordinances from the scroll of Leviticus.

"'These are the regulations for the sin offering: The sin offering is to be slaughtered before the LORD in the place the burnt offering is slaughtered . . .'" Jesus's smooth, young brow wrinkled as he sought the lost words in his memory, his gaze intent on the iron chisel he pounded to create a mortise for the bench they were building.

Joseph positioned his large hands over those of his son and helped him pound the chisel with even strokes to create a deeper cavity in the wood. "'It is most holy.'"

Jesus straightened. "'It is most holy. The priest who offers it shall eat it; it is to be eaten in the sanctuary area.'"

Joseph blinks, chides himself to focus on the task at hand. Finding his son.

"I'm sorry, Mary," Eyal's wife says when they ask after Jesus. "He has not returned to the house."

They thank the woman and head farther into the city. They both know where to look next.

The temple is not as busy as it was the first two days of Passover, when attendance for men was necessary. But many travelers still linger, the sounds of yelling tradesmen mingling with the shouts of water carriers as they offer a drink from skins upon their backs. In the Court of the Gentiles, pilgrims line up at the tables of the money changers or socialize with relatives and neighbors. The pens of the sacrificial animals are empty compared to when Joseph and Mary arrived at the beginning of the feast.

They climb the steps of the Beautiful Gate and enter the Court of Women. It, too, is crowded with people—women worshiping on the two raised daises, patrons placing their offerings in the chests or handing their sacrificial animals to the superintending priest. On Sabbath and feast days such as this one, the scribes teach on the terrace, drawing crowds.

Joseph searches the court, looking for a boy of Jesus's build in his familiar mantle. Nothing. He peers around one of the four large lampstands. Where could his son be? If someone took him . . .

Mary grips Joseph's arm and points toward the wide steps of the Nicanor Gate. "There!"

A *whoosh* of air expels itself from his lungs. They surge forward, weaving through the host of people.

"Jesus!" Mary calls.

But their son's attention is on the teacher at the top of the steps.

"Jesus," Joseph shouts. This time, their son turns his head, his eyes wide when he sees them. He nods respectfully at the teacher before meeting them beside one of the four great lampstands.

Mary throws her arms around him, kisses him, and then squeezes him as though she will never let go. Emotion builds in Joseph's throat, and he wraps his arms around his wife and child.

After a moment, they part. Mary places her hands on Jesus's arms and gazes into his deep brown eyes. "Son, why have you treated us like this? Your father and I have been anxiously searching for you."

"I had questions . . . about the Paschal Lamb, about the offerings. Didn't you know I must be in my Father's house?"

The words are like a millstone in Joseph's stomach. They are drenched with meaning he cannot grasp.

His Father's house? But *he* is Jesus's father. He is the one who encouraged Jesus's first steps and placed the hammer in his hand, who taught him the law and what it means to be a good man—a man of humility who honors HaShem.

As they lead Jesus out of the temple, the whisper of words from many moons ago brushes across his heart.

She will give birth to a son, and you are to give him the name Jesus, because he will save his people from their sins . . .

A light for revelation to the Gentiles, and the glory of your people Israel . . .

The angel's words. Simeon's prophecy. Joseph has not thought on them for some time. Perhaps he has not thought this time would come so soon.

Jesus will go on to do great things for his people. No doubt, this journey to the Holy City has impressed this truth on

Jesus, awakened him to a purpose outside that of a Galilean carpenter's son.

Joseph ushers his wife and son from the temple.

HaShem, help me finish his instruction, to your glory.

Adonai must continue to become more in Jesus's eyes, and perhaps in that knowledge, Joseph must become less.

May it be so.

Reflection Questions

Calling God "Abba" was not common practice until Jesus introduced it. Meditate on Joseph's role in Jesus's life. He is a palpable, necessary part at the beginning and yet by the time of Jesus's crucifixion, he is gone (many speculate he has died). What lessons did Joseph likely impart to his son by the time of this scene at age twelve? What does it mean for you to call God "Father"?

Consider what it might have been like for Jesus to experience the Holy City and the temple. What questions do you think he had for the teachers of the law?

Prayer

Heavenly Father, thank you for your goodness. Not all of us have faithful earthly fathers. Some have caused pain with their actions; some have caused pain with their absence. Help us forgive where necessary. Thank you for being our perfect, eternal Father. When we don't understand the trials of life or even sometimes your ways, may we remember your faithfulness. Amen.

Suggested Reading

Luke 2:41–52

FIVE

The Best for Last

Inspired by John 2:1–12

Aliza focuses her attention on her sandaled feet poking out from the hem of her mantle with each step she takes.

"It's a lovely day for a wedding celebration, is it not?" Her mother gazes at the passing landscape, a road that leads toward the Galilean Sea. Ahead, Aliza glimpses the town of Cana built on a hilly slope, its houses climbing terrace upon terrace.

How can she argue? Weddings are beautiful reasons for celebrations, unless, of course, one is in love with the groom. "It is."

"It is good to have him home." Her mother glances ahead at Aliza's oldest brother, Jesus, her eyes shining.

Aliza understands. While she loves all her brothers and her sister, Jesus brings a security and peace to their home that her heart longs for in his absence. Ever since their father went to be with their ancestors, Jesus has provided for them, directing her brothers in the family business and serving as head of their family.

But Aliza senses a change. Two months ago, Jesus had gone to see John the Immerser in Bethany. He did not say much about what happened after that, but he'd returned to Nazareth only yesterday with a small coterie of disciples in tow. Her brother now has students.

"He will not stay long, will he?" Aliza's voice tremors.

"I am not certain." The corners of her mother's mouth tighten.

Another half mile and they reach the home of Joel ben Eliza, nestled behind the Street of the Wool-Weavers. Music and merriment pour from their friends' home. Joel's mother greets them, and Dalia runs to Aliza. She clasps her best friend's hands, the heaviness in her chest easing. With only a few miles between their homes and their mothers being close friends, Aliza and Dalia spent their childhoods making dolls from straw and bits of fabric from their mothers' sewing baskets. They snuck dates from the cupboards and learned how to grind wheat and spin wool and bake bread. They shared secrets.

All except for one.

Aliza smiles at her friend as she glances around the courtyard of the house. Flowers and torches adorn the outside space. Six large stone pots sit inside the covered galley, which opens to the reception room, the largest room in Dalia's spacious home. "You are expecting a multitude."

Dalia pushes her headscarf over her shoulder to reveal plaited hair wound with silk ribbon. "Abba thought it good business to invite the merchants in the area." Her eyes widen at the sight of Jesus with his small group of followers. "It is true, then? Your brother has taken on the mantle of a rabbi?"

"It would seem so."

"Liza!" Joel strides toward them, handsome in his new tunic and mantle. "I am glad you made it before the procession arrived.

I do not know what I would do without my honorary second sister at my wedding feast."

Aliza fights the heat creeping up her neck. "I would not dream of missing your day."

Joel's gaze alights on Jesus and two of her other brothers. "Excuse me, I must greet the rest of your family."

She watches him go, hoping that seeing Joel married will be the gong of finality her heart needs. It is sinful to long for another woman's husband. She must overcome it. Joel has always viewed her as a little sister; she must put aside fanciful childhood notions.

"It will be us betrothed next," Dalia says on a sigh.

"I cannot think of any I wish to marry."

"You are not thinking hard enough, then." Dalia elbows her. "Wait. I hear the procession—let us go greet Adina."

The bride wears a long veil and embroidered garment, surrounded by her virgin companions. The children of the bridechamber encircle her with myrtle branches, and garlands of flowers adorn her litter. Joel's eyes shine at the sight of his bride.

The couple are decorated with garlands, the ketubah signed. There is the washing of hands and the giving of the benediction and then, finally, the marriage supper commences.

Dalia leads Aliza into the galley, where they use the water in the handsome pots to wash their hands. Tantalizing scents from the kitchen waft toward them. Guests lounge on couches with plush cushions while the bride sits under the huppah. Musicians play lyres and flutes. Men circle the bridegroom in a festive dance. Girls dance and sing. The food arrives from the courtyard kitchen—plates of roast lamb simmering in the juices of wild onions and shallots, salted fish, platters of stuffed dates, sweetmeats flavored with rose and jasmine, honey and raisin cakes, baskets of bread and olive oil, and the wine—plentiful wine! Aliza never knew such a celebration!

The feast lasts long into the night. Guests throw seeds and a crushed pomegranate in front of the couple before they vanish to consummate their marriage. More guests arrive the next day, including some followers of John the Immerser who have come to find Jesus. Joel's parents bask in the praises of their guests. They have honored their family and their son with the beautiful feast. Joel and Adina's marriage will be blessed.

On the sixth day, as some make arrangements to travel home, Aliza notices her mother with Dalia's in the galley with the servants, her face drawn with worry. Aliza has not seen that look since Father died. What could be wrong?

As she inches closer, she hears Dalia's mother speak to the head servant. "I do not understand. We ordered plenty of wine."

"Not enough for the extra guests."

"Extra guests. I do not—" Dalia's mother exchanges a glance with Aliza's mother.

"Jesus," her mother whispers. A proper host would never turn extra guests away. And Jesus had drawn quite a retinue.

"Can we obtain more wine?" Dalia's mother asks the servant.

He shakes his head. "We exhausted the winemaker's stores. His next skins will not be ready for two weeks."

Dalia's mother's face crumbles. "What will we do?"

Aliza's mother meets her gaze. "Find your brother."

Aliza turns and runs from the galley, searching for Jesus in the courtyard. He is not among his followers.

She rushes out of the gates and spots him on the street, speaking with a dirty child. Mindless of propriety, she runs to him. "Jesus!"

He sees her and says something to the child before patting him on the head. The urchin scurries off. Aliza pants from exertion when she reaches her brother. "Ima is asking for you. They have run out of wine."

"I do not see why this involves me." He says the words kindly. Aliza detects a twinkle in his eye.

"Joel will be shamed! This will follow him and Adina all their days, or perhaps Adina's father will accuse him of not being able to provide for his daughter."

Jesus knows this. Why must she explain it to him?

He studies her, those deep brown eyes unwavering from her face. "You care for Joel."

She swallows. He knows. How could he know? She has been careful to hide it. "I do."

"And you wish for his good even if it might bring your heart pain."

Tears prick her eyes. "I do."

He reaches a hand to her elbow, warmth from his fingers traveling up her arm, seeming to take residence in her heart. "Loving without return is real love. You are not far from the kingdom of heaven, my sister."

Aliza follows him up the road toward Joel's house. She watches their mother ask Jesus to help their friends, watches Jesus tell the servants to fill the stone jars used for ceremonial washing with water. She sees lush red wine, about two or three firkins apiece and smelling of earthy fruit, rush out. She hears the master of the banquet declare it the best wine of the feast.

Her spirit lightens. Aliza observes Joel and Adina with surprising joy. How does it not hurt as it did that morning?

She remembers Jesus's hand on her elbow, the familiar warmth she always knows in his presence. She wonders if their mother will agree to allowing her to accompany Jesus on his travels. She can see to the meals and the laundering. She can hear him pray. She can bask in that peaceful presence.

Perhaps someday she will have a husband, but what she really needs is the divine love of Adonai—a love her brother possesses. And she will do anything to be near it.

Reflection Questions

John 2:6 says that Jesus uses water intended for legal purification to turn into wine. This is not only a symbol of God's abundant provision but a first miracle that speaks of the coming of his kingdom. What can you glean about God's kingdom by meditating on this miracle?

We are not told that the servants or even the groom's family came to believe in Jesus from this miracle, but that "his disciples believed in him" (John 2:11). How do you think this miracle served to bolster the faith of those who already placed their trust in Jesus?

Prayer

Gracious Father, thank you for providing not only our daily bread but also, in many ways, a lavish feast for us. Give us eyes to see all that you have offered us. Give us hearts to receive it with gratitude. Amen.

Suggested Reading

John 2:1–12

Isaiah 25:6–8

SIX

At the Synagogue

Inspired by Luke 4:14-30

Ariel stares at the white slab floor of the women's gallery in the synagogue, her skin burning with embarrassment on behalf of the carpenter's son.

This is not what she expected. Jesus ben Joseph had always been a respectful young man. While she had heard about his works as an itinerant rabbi, she had anticipated something different from him today when the hazzan asked him to read from the haphtarah.

She averts her gaze to her mangled foot, which had been caught in a wagon wheel at four years old. She has long grown accustomed to the limp. The cruel jeers of childhood have faded to distant avoidance. She will never marry. And now, with her parents gone to their ancestors, Ariel is alone.

The words of the carpenter's son hang in the air.

"The Spirit of the Lord is on me,
because he has anointed me
to proclaim good news to the poor.
He has sent me to proclaim freedom for the prisoners
and recovery of sight for the blind,
to set the oppressed free,
to proclaim the year of the Lord's favor."

Jesus had always been kind to her—even delivering a word of admonition to her childhood mockers, sharing an emmer cracker with her now and again. But this scroll is one of their town's favorites. Why had Jesus stopped there, in the middle of a line, leaving out the remainder of the words?

The tension in the synagogue could not be cut with the sharpest butcher's knife. Jesus has taken words of judgment and turned them into words of mercy.

Their small town is a proud one. When Aristobulus the Maccabean conquered Galilee and Judaized it, Nazareth became a settler town among Gentiles. Sometimes restless and violent, her people could not accept themselves as a conquered nation. Their hope—a feverish, desperate sort of hope—lay in the prophecies of a savior. A devouring lion. A liberator who would return to defeat the Gentiles and finish what Aristobulus had started.

A Messiah.

This scroll of Isaiah—particularly the latter half—was the core of their history.

And Jesus had ignored it.

Ariel swallows. She has longed for the Messiah more than others, she thinks. For surely, the Messiah would set all to rights. Perhaps even the injustices done her. Perhaps . . . she glances at the wrinkled, deformed flesh of her foot. But no. It will be enough that the Messiah delivers their people from the Romans.

Jesus hands the scroll of Isaiah back to the hazzan and sits down before the men. Quiet blankets the house of prayer. Ariel breathes in the infusion of mint sprinkled on the synagogue floor before service.

"Today this scripture is fulfilled in your hearing." Jesus now speaks in Aramaic instead of the Hebrew used in the reading of the scrolls. There can be no mistaking his words.

A loud hum of excitement breaks the silence. The cheesemaker turns to the man next to him. "Is this not Jesus ben Joseph?"

When they settle, Jesus speaks again, his voice confident, echoing against the palms painted on the stucco walls. "Surely you will quote this proverb to me: 'Physician, heal yourself!' And you will tell me, 'Do here in your hometown what we have heard that you did in Capernaum.'"

Yes! Yes, that is what Ariel wants. Had Jesus, the boy she had seen running in the streets as a child and later discussing the law with the local teachers, healed a leper? If so, would he not be able to do a smaller work of healing her foot?

"Truly I tell you," Jesus continues, "no prophet is accepted in his hometown. I assure you that there were many widows in Israel in Elijah's time, when the sky was shut for three and a half years and there was a severe famine throughout the land. Yet Elijah was not sent to any of them, but to a widow in Zarephath in the region of Sidon. And there were many in Israel with leprosy in the time of Elisha the prophet, yet not one of them was cleansed—only Naaman the Syrian."

The synagogue erupts. Ariel's breaths quicken. The Messiah would come and take their land back from the Gentiles. Why would Jesus claim himself the Messiah at the same time he extols stories of Gentiles coming to faith?

The synagogue ruler stands. "You are a blasphemer!"

But Jesus does not defend himself. Why does he not defend himself?

The hazzan, a teacher, the cheesemaker, and a few other men move toward the carpenter's son and seize him, tearing his prayer shawl from his shoulders and thrusting him toward the door.

"Wait." Ariel turns to the cheesemaker's wife. "Where are they going?"

She sneers at Ariel. "They are taking him outside the town to stone him, of course."

Ariel's throat thickens. She can't breathe. "It is . . . Shabbat."

The cheesemaker's wife shrugs. "Which makes his crime all the worse."

Ariel follows the crowd onto the street. Her foot drags behind in the dirt. Her stride is crooked—her strong leg taking a larger stride than her weaker. What will she accomplish by witnessing Jesus's death? She can do nothing to stop the leaders of the town. Nothing except pray.

By the time she reaches the brow of the hill on which their town is built, she expects to see the men hurling stones off the edge onto Jesus's broken body. She spots Mary, Jesus's mother, and longs to comfort the woman.

But Mary's face shows no sadness. Instead, her eyes are wide, wonder etched upon her features. And then, like the Red Sea before Moses and their ancestors, the crowd is parting, and Jesus walks through it.

Ariel stumbles, catching herself on a large boulder. She watches Jesus walk up the road. The people in the crowd look at one another as if they cannot remember how they came to be on the outskirts of town.

Ariel heads for home, her aching foot making her gait slow. Her mother's kitchen feels empty, not Ariel's to own at all. But she rummages in cabinets for a reed basket. She places the bread she made yesterday inside it along with cheese, a cake of figs, cold lentils, pistachios, and a skin of watered wine.

With the basket on her arm, she starts up the road. Her foot is on fire—the ache all the way to the bone. The many hills of the countryside blur before her but she vows she will do this small thing. It has not been within her means to help another often. But this . . . this she can do.

The first time she discovered the large nook at the base of the ancient, gnarled olive tree, she'd been trying to avoid some cruel boys intent on imitating her limp. The tree had become a haven. But one day soon after, she had found another boy there. The boy Jesus. He had spoken kindly to her. Had made her feel seen, accepted.

Now, when she reaches the spot, she stops short. It is empty.

"Shalom, Ariel," a voice from behind calls.

Tears of relief burn her eyes. She turns and sees the same soulful eyes of his boyhood.

"That basket looks heavy."

She blinks. "I thought you might be hungry."

"You have walked far."

She looks at the ground. "I know it is Shabbat, but I . . . I had to do something."

"I am not scolding you, daughter."

Daughter. She has not thought of herself as a daughter since the death of her parents.

She places the basket down. Jesus sits a few cubits away, beneath the shade of the tree. He prays over the food, and they eat.

"The people did not approve of my words in synagogue this morning."

"No."

"Tell me, what do you think of them?"

Her skin grows hot, but she does not shy away. "Why do you focus on Gentiles?"

He leans back, sighs. "Redemption is for those with true faith, man and woman alike. Those like Naaman the Syrian and the widow of Zarephath. Those who act because of their faith." He takes a bite of date cake. "This lunch is an act of faith."

Her body trembles. "I want to ask that you heal me, but I do not want you to think I have come to you for what you can give."

"Do not fear, Ariel. I see your heart."

And she feels he does. Understanding dawns on her. "You *are* the Messiah."

He smiles, pops a pistachio in his mouth.

They talk for a while longer, and Ariel forgets her food, mesmerized by the words pouring from his lips. She no longer resents that he has withheld the lines about vengeance from the scroll of Isaiah. Instead, she feels love for her Gentile neighbors. Love also for her people—even for those who have treated her unfairly. It does not make sense, but it settles like a warm blanket around her.

When he stands to leave, she does too. But something is different. The familiar pain is gone. She looks down at her foot, new and smooth as a child's. She gasps, but when she looks up, he is gone.

And yet, he is still here, beneath the tree, in the wind, moving within her heart.

Reflection Questions

It would have been easy for Jesus to stand before the people of his hometown and tell them what they wanted to hear, but he does not. In fact, Jesus often speaks hard truths. For what area in your life might you need to listen to a hard truth from God?

The people of Nazareth appear to be most angry that Jesus is not aligning with their picture of what the Messiah should be—someone who will bring vengeance on the Gentiles. And yet, they intend to stone him for blasphemy. What is the danger of forming our religion and politics into a single system of belief?

Prayer

Creator of history past and present, you know where we are apt to stumble. Open our eyes to the parts of us that do not believe with the authentic faith you call us to. Help us look to your grace to inspire us to that faith. Amen.

Suggested Reading

Luke 4:14–30

SEVEN

A Healed Man

Inspired by Mark 1:40-45

He would give anything to touch her again. To be within a few cubits of her, hold a conversation with her. He remembers how she looked the day of their wedding in her new tunic. She smelled of lilies and roses.

Yoram studies her now. From a distance, of course.

Always from a distance.

The law requires it, and he would deny himself tenfold to save her from a fate such as his.

He allows his eyes to roam her face. It is filled with unfamiliar lines—lines that have formed in the three years since he last saw her. Piercing guilt churns his stomach. He is not a perfect man—he knows this. But what sin has he committed that HaShem would bestow upon him such a deadly curse?

He lowers himself behind the dry shrub that hides him from view of his old home. The scent of his fetid skin, rotting off the bone, wafts up to him. The malady has progressed so that it now hurts to walk.

He should not have made the trip. He is more cursed than the ceremonial scapegoat driven from Yerushalayim on the Day of Atonement. But he wanted to see her one time before . . .

"Ima!" A boy of two or three years runs from the house and throws his arms around Yoram's wife. His blood flows hot. She has a son?

The boy turns in his direction. Through the branches of the scrub brush, Yoram's breath catches. He recognizes his own features in the child's—features he used to have, that is.

The boy . . . can it be?

He has a *son*.

He watches the pair for the rest of the day. She washes laundry and sets out figs to dry in the sun. She strikes their olive tree with a long wand and a blessing of ripe olives falls to the ground. His son, whom he hears her call Abram, helps gather the olives. When evening falls, no man comes to the house. Though Yoram is considered dead, and no one would fault her for marrying again, she has not.

The thought causes a fresh surge of love and desperation to flow through him. He must talk with them. He must meet his son.

He stands on painful feet and steps from the brush. Her name is on his lips, but not before the scene plays out before him. Her horror at his appearance—his rotting hands and lionish face. Or perhaps she would come to him even though the law forbids it. And what of his son? The boy named Abram would cower behind his mother's mantle at the sight of him. Would the single memory he offers his child be one of horror?

He swallows disappointment and turns away. There is no hope. No hope, unless . . . he remembers what he heard on the road to his old home. A rabbi from Capernaum was said to heal many, including a man with an impure spirit. If the rumors are true . . .

He has nothing to lose. His feet may not endure the journey, but if he must languish on the road, it will be no worse than his fate at the leper community near Samaria. He turns toward Capernaum, his heart aching at the sound of his wife's sweet alto voice singing their son a lullaby.

Twelve Days Later

Yoram shuffles toward the crowd, a painful fire aflame in his feet. The heat moves upward. He ripped strips from his tunic to pad his soles, but the skin chafes with each step; infection has set in. The fever began last night. Every time he hears news of the rabbi, it seems he has arrived too late. There is little time left.

He pushes nearer. But his feet can bear no more. He falls to his knees, crawling closer . . . closer still. "Rabbi!"

Those on the outskirts of the crowd recoil at the sight of him. They wrinkle their noses at the scent of his festering flesh. He is breaking the law. Any minute, they will throw stones at him. But he can't turn away. Not when he is so close.

A few people stumble off the road, allowing him to glimpse a man who is different from the rest of them. Not because of his appearance or clothing but because he is walking *toward* him instead of away from him.

Yoram pushes himself forward with scraped knees, presses his forehead to the ground. "Rabbi, if you are willing, make me clean."

There is a moment of silence, but Yoram does not lift his head—cannot bear to think of this man's rejection of him.

But then—a gentle touch upon his head, the human contact both foreign and welcome.

"I am willing. Be clean!"

Before he comprehends the words, Yoram feels a difference in his body. It is as if the pain seeps away into the ground beneath him, as if he has been made new and alive with strength. He blinks, lifts his head.

He glances at his hand. White flesh no longer rots off bone. His skin appears smooth—like that of a newborn babe's. His vision is clear. He unwinds the bandages from his feet and wiggles his toes, laughs at the spryness of them, at the new skin that has formed.

He laughs again. He cannot contain the joy bubbling up within him. He stands and throws his arms around the rabbi. "Thank you. Thank you!" Then he falls to the man's feet and clasps his ankles. "Thank you!"

The rabbi bids him rise. "Listen, my son. See that you don't tell this to anyone. But go, show yourself to the priest and offer the sacrifices that Moses commanded for your cleansing, as a testimony to them."

Yoram nods and once more expresses his gratitude before scurrying away. He will seek out the priests. He will offer the sacrifices. And then he will return home to his wife. To his *son*. But be silent? How can he not tell everyone he knows about what this man has done for him?

Reflection Questions

Some of the laws surrounding leprosy were associated with tracing the disease to moral shortcomings. What is the harm in associating sickness and unfortunate circumstances with an individual's sin? How does this negate the doctrine of original sin?

This man comes to Jesus not only out of faith but out of a complete and hopeless need. How are we like this man in our approach to Jesus? How are we different?

Prayer

Gracious God, thank you for being willing to touch the dirty parts of our hearts. Thank you for not abandoning us in our pride, in our transgressions, in our hunger for the meaningless things of this world. Help us realize our need for you. May we be filled with your grace that we may go forward to love you and our fellow humans. Amen.

Suggested Reading

Mark 1:40–45

EIGHT

Take Your Mat

Inspired by Mark 2:1–12

He is not as confident as the men who carry him on his mat. He is not so certain that Jesus of Nazareth will heal him.

Uri's body sways from side to side as his father, his uncle, his cousin, and his newly married best friend Benjamin carry him through the thickening crowd.

"Jesus will have you good as new, eh?" Benjamin says. "You will be beating me at our footraces again by nightfall."

Uri does not answer, only stares at his lifeless legs arranged in front of him.

Jesus *can* heal him, but will he? Uri heard of the healings the rabbi performed last summer. But had all those Jesus healed been burdened by such sin as Uri?

Transgressions hindered healing. What hope was there for him, then?

The crowd grows dense as they draw near Peter's home. Uri's father works for Zebedee, whose sons left the family fishing business to follow Jesus.

The men lower Uri to the ground a distance from the crowd. The ropes they use to carry him lay limp in the dirt.

So many. So many to see the teacher.

"I will search for him." Uri's father gives an unspoken request for the others to stay by Uri's side, to protect him from passing carts and foot traffic, to watch out for him.

Always to watch out for him.

He thought, at the age of nineteen, that he'd be watching out for himself. A provider, a protector for a wife and, perhaps one day, children. But that had changed seventeen months ago when he'd thrown himself in front of a Roman's horse to save his friend.

Benjamin lowers himself beside Uri's mat and places a firm hand on his shoulder. "You deserve for this to happen, Uri. You deserve to be healed." Benjamin blinks. "I know I should be on this mat. You should be marrying *your* sweetheart, expecting *your* first child." His voice catches.

"Stop," Uri manages. "I do not regret my actions."

And he doesn't. Yes, Benjamin had been foolish to taunt that clean-shaven Roman, but Uri hadn't paused when he'd seen the giant horse rear up on the soldier's orders. A flash of a red cloak, a cuirass, and flailing hooves. He'd rushed to push Benjamin out of the way. The hard hooves had landed on Uri's back instead.

"I regret mine." Benjamin presses his lips together. They have not spoken like this in months. It is too painful. Besides, Benjamin's presence stirs something ugly in him, causing Uri to break the tenth commandment repeatedly—to covet not only Benjamin's health but his very life.

How can he expect God to forgive such intense covetousness?

His father walks around the crowd, then back in their direction. "There is no way through."

Benjamin stands, scanning the multitude, his gaze traveling to the roof. "Where is he teaching?"

His father squints, as if he can see through the throng. "From what I can tell, he is in the western part of the covered gallery. The crowd spills onto the streets from the courtyard."

Benjamin places bunched fists on his hips. He is a carpenter by trade—his own father likely built this very home. "We cannot wait."

"Please, take me home," Uri says. This is humiliating. He prefers to stay home if he can help it. Now, people stare. Even the scribes at the edge of the crowd eye him with suspicion. They know why he is here. What they do not know is how little he believes the rabbi will heal him.

"No. We did not bring you all this way to turn back." Benjamin's strong will is why Uri is on this mat to begin with.

"Take me home," Uri demands, hating his helplessness anew.

Benjamin's eyes light up. "I have an idea."

In moments, despite Uri's protests, they round the house and carry him up the stairs to the roof. He leans awkwardly back on the mat, gripping the ropes to keep from sliding off and embarrassing himself further.

"What are you planning?" Uri's cousin asks.

Benjamin leads them beyond the washing spread out to dry and toward the west roof of the covered gallery. After they lower him, his friend peers over the three-foot balustrade into the courtyard and measures with his footsteps back in their direction, stopping short a few cubits from Uri's mat. His eyes shine.

In that moment, Uri realizes Benjamin needs this healing as much as Uri does. Could it be possible? Perhaps Jesus will not know of Uri's sins. Perhaps he will heal him despite his transgressions.

Hope builds in his chest, and he tries to tamp it down. "This is a fool's errand, Benjamin."

But his friend shakes his head. "Jesus is below us. The roof here above the gallery is more mud and thatch than brick and stone. We will dig through it."

His cousin blanches. "Ruin Peter's home?"

"I can repair it later without much trouble. Is Uri not worth it?"

Uri's father nods. "Show me what to do."

Uri's heart thrums as they dig with their hands. The mud and thatch of the roof are crumbly and dry. This is mad. What if Peter chastises them and orders them away? What if Jesus is appalled at their audacity and refuses to look at him?

He hears the gasps from the crowd as they realize what his companions intend. Jesus has stopped teaching, no doubt rained upon by bits of dirt.

"Ready?" Benjamin asks when they've finally made a hole big enough to stuff him through. "The ropes are long enough for us to lower you."

Uri chafes at the idea of being dropped into a potentially hostile situation all by himself, but they have gone through much trouble. What choice does he have other than to throw himself at the feet of Jesus?

Carefully, they lower Uri through the roof. He clings to the wobbling mat and avoids the dozens of eyes upon him. Finally, he feels solid, beaten earth beneath him. He raises his gaze to the rabbi.

The man looks at Uri with a tenderness he does not expect. And yet it lacks pity—it is as if Jesus sees all of him, as if there is no hiding. The rabbi looks up at Uri's father and cousin and friend on the roof, a small smile tugging at the corners of his mouth.

He then gazes at Uri. "Child, your sins are forgiven."

Uri shakes his head. How? How does Jesus know this is what he needs—perhaps more than the ability to walk?

It is as if a shackle falls from his chest, as if his great sin of covetousness has been lifted from him. He is light, unburdened. He is so filled with joy he hardly hears Jesus chastising the teachers of the law.

"Which is easier: to say to this paralyzed man, 'Your sins are forgiven,' or to say, 'Get up, take your mat and walk'? But I want you to know that the Son of Man has authority on earth to forgive sins." He turns to Uri. "I tell you, my son, get up, take your mat, and go home."

The lightness in Uri's chest travels to his thighs, to his knees, and to the muscles of his calves and toes. Foreign sensation courses through his blood. He moves the big toe of his right foot. He laughs, gasping as his knee bends. He looks to Jesus, who nods, his eyes twinkling. In moments, it is as if that Roman horse had never landed on his back. He is standing—he is *walking!*

Above him, his father and Benjamin cheer and hug one another, brushing tears from their faces.

Uri throws his arms around Jesus, words of gratitude pouring forth. He picks up his mat and pushes through the amazed crowd. His father and Benjamin meet him in the courtyard, and he hugs them, realizing for the first time he is now taller than his father.

His life has changed in moments. Because of Jesus, because of his family and friend. He did nothing. He had little faith. All he brought were his sins, and Jesus had taken care of it all.

Reflection Questions

It is interesting to note that Jesus forgives the paralyzed man's sins before he requests it. The cross heralds forgiveness even before we ask. How can we respond to God's grace in this manner?

Jesus does not initially focus on the property damage or even the man in front of him, but on the faith of those who brought the paralyzed man to him. Their faith in action seems to prompt not only the forgiving of the man's sins but the healing. What do you make of this order? What does this tell us about the value God places on caregivers?

Prayer

Forgiving Father, thank you for initiating our relationship with you. Give us a faith like those who carried the paralyzed man to you. May we so love our fellow hurting humans that we are willing to carry them to you with gentle hands. Grant us courage when needed or wisdom and restraint when needed. Thank you for your overwhelming love and grace.

Suggested Reading

Matthew 9:1–7

Mark 2:1–12

Luke 5:17–26

NINE

A Secret Belief

Inspired by John 3:1–21

He is not hiding.

At least, this is what Nicodemus tells himself as he travels through the dark, narrow streets of Yerushalayim with his robes tucked securely around him.

The wind brushes his face, and he pushes into it, hastening to his destination. This visit is ill-advised, but he cannot turn around. He cannot deny the signs. He cannot deny the strange stirring that pulls forth simultaneous feelings of fear and wonder.

The questions burn within him—he cannot sleep, he cannot focus on the rituals of the recent Passover Feast or his duties as chief of the bet ha-midrash.

He *must* settle his mind. And this nighttime visit is the only way to do so.

John ben Zebedee waits for him at the bottom of the stairs that lead to the guestchamber on the roof of the lodgings the fisherman stays in while in Yerushalayim.

John greets him with the secrecy one might expect on such a night. "He is upstairs. Follow me."

Nicodemus swallows and obeys. He feels like a boy at his first day of Torah school—uncertain and out of place, the folds of his mother's robe left far behind. In this instance, the folds of the law, of everything he thought he knew about HaShem, seem to fade into the distance with each stair he climbs.

He should turn back. What is he thinking, looking to this untrained Galilean as a teacher from HaShem? The people to the north are lax in their observation of the law. They are a poor, uneducated bunch, surrounded by many nations and unbelievers. What would his peers think of him?

And yet, is it not his duty, as an esteemed teacher and one of seventy members of the Sanhedrin, to seek out the meaning behind the miracles and signs?

He reaches the roof, where a single lamp illuminates a figure at a table in the far corner. John melts into the darkness. Nicodemus approaches the man named Jesus.

The Galilean smiles. "Sit, my friend."

The gesture and title, said through the obvious accent of his people, catches Nicodemus off guard. While Nicodemus is accustomed to the eager courtesy and deference given to his station, Jesus did not go out of his way to gain his audience. As with everything else, the Galilean proves himself unlike others. Without pretense, without haughty airs. He is simply here. Calm, peaceful, still.

Nicodemus lowers himself into the chair across from Jesus. "Thank you for seeing me."

Jesus nods.

Nicodemus clears his throat. "Rabbi, we know that you are a teacher who has come from God. For no one could perform the signs you are doing if God were not with him."

The man studies him. Nicodemus shifts in his seat, unaccustomed to such blatant examination.

"Very truly, I tell you," Jesus says, "no one can see the kingdom of God without being born from above."

Nicodemus raises his eyebrows. What can he mean? The kingdom of God is for those in Abraham's line. And as far as being born from above, surely that includes one such as himself—a married rabbi, head of the rabbinical school. He's done everything possible to be born from above!

"But Rabbi, how can someone be born when they are an old man like me? Surely, they cannot enter a second time into their mother's womb to be born!" He laughs at the absurdity. Their people already possess Abraham's covenant. What more is there?

Jesus leans forward, and Nicodemus finds himself doing the same. The younger man's brown eyes shine beside the lamp, intense and genuine. "Very truly I tell you, Nicodemus, no one can enter the kingdom of God unless they are born of water and the Spirit. Flesh gives birth to flesh, but the Spirit gives birth to spirit." He shifts in his chair. "You should not be surprised at my saying, 'You must be born from above.' The wind blows wherever it pleases. You hear its sound, but you cannot tell where it comes from or where it is going. So it is with everyone born of the Spirit."

The words swirl in Nicodemus's mind. A cricket chirps outside and a brush of wind comes through the window, as if to spur understanding to life.

But he does not understand. Unbidden, the prophet Ezekiel's words come to him.

I will sprinkle clean water on you, and you will be clean. . . . I will give you a new heart and put a new spirit in you. . . . I will put my Spirit in you . . .

Nicodemus wants God's Spirit, of course, but how can he possess it without understanding?

"How can this be?" he whispers.

"You are Israel's teacher," Jesus says, "and do you not understand these things? Very truly I tell you, we speak of what we know, and we testify to what we have seen, but still you people do not accept our testimony. I have spoken to you of earthly things and you do not believe; how then will you believe if I speak of heavenly things?"

He understands what entering the kingdom means, but the how . . . that remains a mystery.

Jesus continues. "No one has ever gone into heaven except the one who came from heaven—the Son of Man. Just as Moses lifted up the snake in the wilderness, so the Son of Man must be lifted up, that everyone who believes may have eternal life in him."

Nicodemus blinks. The uplifted serpent had brought life to those who gazed upon it. Jesus was saying the Son of Man would give life to those who gaze upon him.

The Son of Man.

Slowly, he meets Jesus's gaze.

"You see, Nicodemus, do you not? For God so loved the world that he gave his one and only Son, that whoever believes in him shall not perish but have eternal life. For God did not send his Son into the world to condemn the world, but to save the world through him."

Jesus's words fade as Nicodemus finally grasps what Jesus is saying. What Jesus is saying about himself.

Nicodemus was wrong to think this visit would settle his mind. Instead, it has set it afire.

Now, what is he to do with it all?

Reflection Questions

Nicodemus's visit with Jesus upended many of his expectations. How do you think he processed this new information? Do you think his belief came quickly or with time?

How can some of our own cultural Christian expectations hinder us from drawing closer to Jesus?

Prayer

Heavenly Father, there is great blessing in the mystery of who you are. Thank you for revealing to us the things we need to know about you. Thank you for humbling us to understand there are some things we may never know. Lord, help us to seek after you with childlike faith, to bask in what you've given us, and to be content with resting in the mystery of that which you have not yet revealed.

Suggested Reading

John 3:1–21

TEN

Thirsting for More

Inspired by John 4:1-30

The sturdy wooden pole rests heavy across her shoulders, but she is accustomed to the weight of the water buckets as she travels to and from the well at the sixth hour of each day.

She is not, however, accustomed to seeing a group of Galilean men, proud tassels swinging at the hems of their garments.

They do not move off the olive tree–lined path, and though her insides bristle, she steps off the road into the tall grass to make way for them. And why shouldn't she? Her entire life, after all, has been about making way for men.

The Jews pass without acknowledging her, and she continues on, climbing the ridge between Mount Gerizim and Mount Ebal. The trees give way to bright noonday sun shining down on whitened wheat.

Sagmi groans at the sight of another Galilean man sitting on the capstone of the well. Her only peace in the middle of her day, and now it is ruined.

But this is *her* land. This dappled country, whispering promises of wheat. This home of passage, where Barak answered Deborah's call and defeated Sisera.

Why should she be deterred? Sagmi stands still, waiting. The weight of the water buckets triggers a kink in her neck. Why did the man on the capstone not withdraw the appropriate thirteen cubits to allow her to continue forward?

She scowls. Sweat bunches at her breastbone and beneath her tunic. She steps forward, but the man still does not move. Never mind, then. He will be the one worried about contaminating himself. She will not allow one man to ruin her plans. She has tasks to accomplish. She must return to Zusman—the man she lives with does not approve of her lingering at the well.

She lifts the wooden pole from her neck and lowers the pails to the dirt. The Galilean still sits!

Sagmi exhales and unrolls the small leather bucket attached to her belt. Crossed sticks at the mouth of the container keep it open to fill. She attaches it to the rope and lowers it, jiggling it to allow the water to rush in.

She ignores the man as she leans over the capstone built to keep dirt from blowing into the well. It blocks children and animals from falling in and gives her a place to fill her buckets.

It was not built for Galileans to sit upon.

"Will you give me a drink?" The man's accent is unmistakable.

Sagmi glances up sharply.

Is he mocking her? Jewish men do not often speak to their wives in public, never mind a Samaritan woman. And to ask her for something? Does this man want more than water from her?

She pulls her bucket, now brimming with cool water, from the well and sets it on the stone in front of him. The man's brow glistens in the sun as he drinks. Could he simply be thirsty? Simply be forgetting his holy pride in a time of need?

The lengthy history between her people and the Jews goes back to the Babylonian captivity. Her people had been left behind, so they intermarried with Gentiles. When the Jews returned to their homeland, they shunned the Samaritans, forcing them to build their own temple on Mount Gerizim. But over a century ago, the Jews had burned it, instilling fresh hatred on both sides.

"Thank you." He slides the small bucket back in her direction but makes no move to get up.

She swallows. Why isn't he leaving now that she has given him what he wanted, as most men in her life tend to do? "You are a Jew, and I am a Samaritan woman. How can you ask me for a drink?"

The man swipes at his brow. "If you knew the gift of God and who it is that asks you for a drink, you would have asked him, and he would have given you living water."

Sagmi laughs. This man has been in the sun too long. "Sir, you have nothing to draw with and the well is deep. Where can you get this living water?" She does not bother to curb her mocking tone. This is the well of *her* people. This place belongs to *her* ancestors. "Are you greater than our father Jacob, who gave us this well and drank from it himself, as did also his sons and his livestock?"

"Everyone who drinks this water will be thirsty again, but whoever drinks the water I give will never thirst. Indeed, the water I give them will become in them a spring of water welling up to eternal life."

She hungers at his words. It is the same glimpse of peace she sometimes senses when she visits the well, an impossible notion that there is still hope for her.

"Sir, give me this water so that I will not get thirsty and have to keep coming here to draw water."

He nods. "Go, call your husband and come back."

Sagmi blinks. The request is not an altogether unusual one. This man is already pushing the boundaries of what is proper.

"I have no husband." It is the truth. He need not know the details.

He meets her gaze. "You are right when you say you have no husband. The fact is, you have had five husbands, and the man you now have is not your husband. What you have just said is quite true."

The rope slides from her fingers.

How can he know? What is more, she senses he knows *all*. That Michael, her first love and the man of her heart, died in the second year of their marriage. That her second husband, Lior, divorced her because she had not produced a child for him. That her third husband, an older man named Ezra, had died also without giving her a child. Then she was forced to marry Ezra's widowed brother, and something shriveled inside her. After he died, she stopped caring and allowed herself to become bitter. This man knows she allowed lust to get the better of her when she met an interested foreigner at this very well, and when he left, she sought the shelter of Zusman's home, not caring about a formal marriage contract if it meant having a roof above her head.

"Sir, I can see you are a prophet. Our ancestors worshiped on this mountain, but you Jews claim that the place we must worship is in Yerushalayim."

Yes, she avoids his comment. Better to bait him with political talk—all the men she knows forget everything when preoccupied with the long-standing hatred between the Jews and the Samaritans.

"Woman, believe me, a time is coming when you will worship the Father neither on this mountain nor in Yerushalayim."

She stops pulling up the bucket to drink in his words. For as long as she can remember, she has been told that Mount Gerizim, the hill the waters of the flood had never covered, was the true mountain of worship. But now, the temple is gone. How lovely to *not* be dependent on a certain place to draw near to HaShem!

He continues. "You Samaritans worship what you do not know; we worship what we do know, for salvation is from the Jews. Yet a time is coming and has now come when the true worshipers will worship the Father in the Spirit and in truth, for they are the kind of worshipers the Father seeks. God is spirit, and his worshipers must worship in the Spirit and in truth."

He speaks of what her heart longs for, what is just out of her grasp. He speaks of what it might mean to belong. "I know that the Messiah is coming. When he comes, he will explain everything to us."

He waits until she again meets his gaze. "I, the one speaking to you—I am he."

The unsettled part of her spirit slides into place.

I am he.

This man . . . this man is the Messiah! And he has chosen to reveal himself to her—a Samaritan sinner, and a woman at that!

Has HaShem not abandoned her after all? Was he opening a way for her to be with him that didn't involve a temple?

Like a bubbling spring, joy gurgles up within her, and she stumbles back, her water jar forgotten. She holds her hand up to the man sitting on the well. "Please, do not leave. I must tell the others."

She turns and flies down the hill, hope unspooling within her. The Messiah is here! He will make everything right again.

She had gone to the well to draw water that would sate her for a few hours. Now, she leaves, having drunk of the living water that will satisfy her thirst forever.

Reflection Questions

How does Jesus upset cultural expectations in this story regarding whom he reveals himself to?

The Samaritan woman finds that the greatest gift of God is not a place or a book but Jesus. Imagine how she felt running back to her town.

Prayer

Father of all people and all creation, thank you for giving us not only our daily bread but spiritual food and drink that fill our souls. May we be as eager as the Samaritan woman to share your love with the world. Amen.

Suggested Reading

John 4:1–42

ELEVEN

The Worthiness of a Tax Collector

Inspired by Mark 2:13–17, Matthew 9:9–13, and Luke 18:9–14

Matthew gazes at the blood of the lamb smeared on the great high altar of the temple. The trumpets blow and cymbals clash, signaling the atonement offering for God's people—the only way for them to draw near to his presence.

He thinks of his seaside village of Capernaum. He thinks of the flat-roofed houses, olive orchards, and fields of grain. Of the carob tree with its hanging bunches of red flowers, of the customs house by the sea where he takes taxes from the ships coming into port, ensuring that each import is paid for, that Rome will gather every shekel they demand.

And ensuring, of course, that he is paid adequately as well.

He swallows around the walnut-sized lump in his throat as the priest reads one of the psalms. Why has he come to Yerushalayim for the Passover celebration? There is no repentance great enough nor atonement pure enough to make him right before HaShem.

The priest disappears inside the Holy Place, and several moments later, the scent of frankincense and spikenard surrounds the court. The men in the court pray, but Matthew cannot form even one word. Emotion builds in his throat.

There is no hope. For his people, yes, but not for him.

A sure, confident voice comes from several cubits away. Ananias, a teacher from Capernaum. They traveled to the Holy City in the same caravan. "Adonai, I thank you that I am not like other people—robbers, evildoers, adulterers—or even like this tax collector."

Matthew's face burns. Most in Yerushalayim are not aware of his choices, but now all in the temple court will know he is unclean. They will know why the Pharisee has chosen to stand apart from him.

Ananias continues. "I fast twice a week and give a tenth of all I get."

Matthew keeps his head bowed. He thinks of the lavish house he bought for himself, of his fine clothes and daily food and drink. Of the generous portion he keeps when he gathers money from the incoming ships.

Despair wraps around him, chafing like a camel hair blanket. He can't even look up to heaven. He is so unworthy. He belongs with the trash, destined to be burned outside the city.

He thinks about his life as a boy, how he longed to be taught under a great rabbi—maybe Rabbi Johanan or Rabbi Hanina. But he'd never been chosen by an elite teacher or even a mediocre one. Instead, his skill with numbers caught the eye of a local gabbai. The tax gatherer had believed in his ability, had taught him and invested time in him when no rabbi would.

But in this moment, Matthew would give it all up if that blood on the altar could be meant for him too. He beats his chest, doesn't care that the gesture is usually one for mourning women. He deserves to be shamed. Deserves to feel the curse of his sin—the sin of greed, the sin of betraying his people. HaShem's people.

Words erupt in his throat. He cannot bring his good deeds to the Lord. He has nothing to bring. "HaShem, have mercy on me, a sinner."

Two Months Later

There is an excitement layering the air in Capernaum of late, and Matthew is not immune to it. A rabbi from Nazareth by the name of Jesus ben Joseph has performed strange signs and miracles. Not only had he healed a leper and driven out an evil spirit in the synagogue last Shabbat but Matthew himself has seen the much-talked-about rabbi call fishermen—the feisty Simon, his brother Andrew, and even the sons of Zebedee—to be his students. Matthew had gone to bet sefer with them.

The twinge of jealousy Matthew felt at seeing the rabbi call to the rough, uneducated men had lasted only a moment. He had business to attend to. Taxes to oversee—ground taxes, bridge money, harbor dues, road taxes, town taxes—and directing of the imports and exports. He could not think about such things as a new rabbi in town.

But then the centurion Decimus told Matthew of Jesus healing his servant without even touching him. This rabbi had tended to the affairs of a Roman!

Something in Matthew's gut leaped at the notion. What would this teacher do next?

He was not the only one with the question, which was why white-sailed ships cast themselves on the Sea of Galilee alongside fishing dories and flat-bottomed barges. Most were not coming to Capernaum to bring their imports; they were coming to see Jesus of Nazareth.

Matthew turns from the sea and walks to his customs booth, where he sits and watches the visitors coming to shore. Will they find the rabbi at Simon's house that evening?

"Matthew!" He startles at the sound of his name. Recognizes the voice—the object of his thoughts. But it can't be . . . how does the rabbi know his name?

"Rabbi?" Matthew turns, his voice small and tinny, not his own at all.

"Follow me!"

He knocks his chest. "M-me?"

"Yes! Come, follow me."

After all these years, he would be the student of a rabbi? And not just any rabbi—a rabbi who made paralyzed men walk and healed lepers?

He glances at his booth, knows there will be consequences for leaving it, and yet it does not matter. Not with that voice calling *him*.

He latches the door, ignoring the surprised, annoyed looks of the fishermen surrounding Jesus.

"You must come to my house. I will have my servants prepare a feast." He has nothing to offer this teacher but this. Perhaps it will be enough.

Two hours later, Matthew's fine house is filled with his tax collector friends, with friends and family of the four fishermen, with the aimless wanderers on the street. It is glorious.

When Matthew sees the Pharisee Ananias at his gate conferring with his peers, he does not care about that day at the temple. He only wishes to share his joy. "Ananias! Come inside and bring your friends!"

The Pharisee gives him a look of derision. Matthew has changed, but perhaps the world has not.

"Why does your teacher eat with tax collectors and sinners?" Ananias calls from a distance.

That's right. He and his friends are unclean. Ananias will not come near.

But Jesus comes out of the house. He draws near to Ananias. "It is not the healthy who need a doctor, but the sick," he says. "But go and learn what this means: 'I desire mercy, not sacrifice.' For I have not come to call the righteous, but sinners."

The words spin like fine silk in Matthew's soul. This rabbi—*his* rabbi—is turning everything on its head. As Ananias and the others walk away, Jesus turns to Matthew.

"I saw you that day in the temple."

He remembers how he beat his chest. He remembers the shame of the moment, the sorrow of his choices. And yet this rabbi saw it all. He sees him.

What's more, despite it all, he *chose* him.

Reflection Questions

Read the parable of the Pharisee and the tax collector (Luke 18:9–14). What does this parable tell us about how we are made right with God?

How do you think Matthew felt when he heard Jesus say, "For I have not come to call the righteous, but sinners" (Matt. 9:13)?

Prayer

Father, I can see myself in both of these extremes—the self-righteous Pharisee and the repentant sinner who recognizes the depth of their need for you. Turn my heart to you, that I would understand the extent of my sin but forever keep my eyes on you, my Savior. Lord, have mercy on me, a sinner. Amen.

Suggested Reading

Matthew 9:9–13

Luke 18:9–14

TWELVE

Widow of Nain

Inspired by Luke 7:11–17

She cannot bear the weight of this grief. When her husband, Hiram, died three years ago, the sorrow, though great, was not this immense, this cavernous, this deep. With her only child on his way to his ancestors, she has been robbed of her last worldly hope.

She follows the funeral orator, his lips proclaiming the good deeds of her sixteen-year-old son. Behind her, Caleb's friends bear the weight of the bier. He has been carefully laid in the wickerwork, his hair and nails cut, his body washed and anointed with spikenard and myrrh. She had wrapped him in the finest linen she possessed and folded his hands on his breast. Beside him, she had tucked the pen and ink set Hiram gifted him at the age of six. She had woven a garland of myrtle through the wicker, its honeyed, herbaceous scent doing nothing now to soothe her grieving spirit.

The moans of the mourning women echo strains of lament from behind. Tears cascade down her cheeks. Caleb will never again enter their home, his face beaming, his hands eager for the breadbasket. She will never again see him tucked over the table with pen and ink, studying the prophecies of old. She still remembers him as a youth, begging her to shovel a bit of ash from the oven so he could mix it with tree sap and water to make his ink. It does not seem possible he is gone, for her son had been so full of life and love. But indeed, the angel of death had placed the drop of bitter gall between Caleb's lips, stealing his breath of life and causing the scandalous shadow of death to fall upon him.

Fresh tears leak from her eyes, and her throat closes with emotion. If only it would close forever and take her breath, if only she could escape with Caleb and Hiram to the place of their ancestors and skip this time of shiva altogether.

They approach the gate and head east toward the burying ground. People have come out of their homes and businesses along the way to show respect for her loss and throw dust upon their hair. The despondent clink of cymbals and music of melancholy flutes float around them. She is touched by these people, but not even her friends can comfort her now.

She lifts wet eyes to the view before her—a view Caleb loved. He cherished their small town of Nain, built high on a hill, spreading forth a glorious view of purple vineyards and tawny deserts across the plain of Carmel and into the hills of Nazareth. The white cap of Mount Hermon glistens in the distance.

The orator calls out. "Weep with him, all you who are bitter of heart!"

More tears. Will she ever know anything but this lonely grief that twists and wears at her soul? A mother is not meant to bury the one she brought into life.

She senses an approaching figure nearby but hardly cares to look up. She cannot see through her tears anyhow. Perhaps the orator is directing someone entering the town gate to fall into line behind the rest of the mourners. What does it matter? What does any of it matter?

"Don't cry." The voice is clear and kind. She looks up, ready to shed fresh tears at this man who dares to defile her son's right to an honorable burial. Then the man passes her. He reaches out a workworn hand to touch the wicker of the bier.

The action is incomprehensible. He makes himself unclean. He interrupts this most sacred of ceremonies.

Caleb's friends stand still beneath the weight of the bier, mesmerized by the stranger. She, too, is captivated by his actions, captivated by him. Again, he speaks. "Young man, I say to you, get up!"

She blinks. What is this man thinking with his cruelty? He is mocking her and the memory of her son with such blatant disrespect.

The depths of her grief cause her to question the slight movement atop the bier. How many times, as she prepared her son's body, did she imagine such a thing? Imagine that he found the breath of life the sickness had stolen?

But then . . . the unthinkable! Caleb is sitting up, looking around in confusion at his friends holding his bier. His brow wrinkles. His face is full of color and life.

She falls to her knees. It cannot be. Her Caleb—he is speaking!

"Nathan? Samuel? What is this about? Where is my mother?"

Those in the funeral procession gasp, their shock rippling down the road as they comprehend what she still does not. Her son . . . is alive?

Caleb's friends set the bier on the ground and the stranger helps him out of the wicker basket. Her son has a myrtle leaf in his hair, and she reaches out as if to touch it, to touch him.

The stranger helps her up, guiding her into Caleb's arms. She collapses into them, sobbing with disbelief and hope. When she parts from her son, she stares at the stranger. He is plain-looking in a worn tunic and mantle. "Thank you, sir. Thank you! Certainly, you are a great prophet."

"God has come to help his people!" Caleb's friend Nathan declares.

And with the joy coursing through her, the widow of Nain cannot argue with such a statement.

Reflection Questions

This event occurred "soon after" Jesus healed a centurion's servant in Capernaum. What is the importance of the attention Jesus gives to both a grieving Gentile man and a grieving Jewish mother?

The link between the crowd that follows Jesus (symbolizing life) and the crowd that follows the grieving mother (symbolizing death) is the deep distress of the Jewish mother. We are told that "when the Lord saw her, his heart went out to her" (Luke 7:13). How can this story comfort us in times of grief and sorrow?

Prayer

Heavenly Father, you tell us that in your upside-down kingdom those who mourn will be blessed. Help us take the time to grieve when needed. God of comfort, be with us in our sorrow.

Give us the courage and wisdom to console those who mourn. And Lord, may we bring your peace and life into every dark space and corner of death we meet. Amen.

Suggested Reading

Luke 7:11–17

THIRTEEN

The Anointed

Inspired by Luke 7:36–50

She still cannot comprehend what has happened. There is an excitement in her alongside an unexplainable peace, a demanding hunger alongside a curious satisfaction.

She, Devorah the prostitute, has been forgiven.

Jesus's words spoken in front of the town synagogue echo within her.

Come to me, all you who are weary and burdened, and I will give you rest.

In the midst of the crowd, his eyes had landed on her. *That* was how she felt! Weary and burdened.

She has been with many men. She is a sinner. But the priests and teachers of the law, with their careful attempts to cross the street when they glimpse her, discourage her from seeking their help.

Did they think she enjoyed the attentions of so many men, being used and wrung out like a well-worn dishrag, bearing the yoke of shame and sorrow? As a girl, she dreamed of being a heroine of Israel, like Esther. But such dreams are vapor. After Asa divorced her and spread those wretched rumors to distract from the fact that he himself had been unfaithful, she had no choice. No man wanted her. And so, she stepped into the story everyone already believed. Better to live as a woman of sin than die alone, without family or children to comfort her.

Still, it is a tasteless, painful business—the giving away of her body and the keeping of men's secrets in exchange for coin.

But now . . . now there is hope.

Take my yoke upon you and learn from me, for I am gentle and humble in heart, and you will find rest for your souls. For my yoke is easy and my burden is light.

She has been *forgiven*. A liberating tune played across her spirit at Jesus's words. She feels like a slave set free in the Year of Jubilee. How can she express her gratitude?

She tugs her headscarf tightly around her, the gesture causing the small flask of perfume beneath her tunic to move against her heart. The teacher is to share a meal with Simon the Pharisee tonight. It is bold for her to go, but how can she stay away? How can she not seek out this man, Jesus of Nazareth, who has paved a new way for her?

When Simon sees her, he folds his arms in front of his robes, the tzitzit on the hems particularly long above his embroidered sandals. She stops well away from him, bows her head in deference. She will not humiliate him by speaking to him, but her request is plain. She only wishes to occupy a corner. She will not touch anyone or anything, not even the mezuzah fixed to the threshold. She will not take a bite of food. She only wants to be near the prophet.

"You are not welcome here." Simon's teeth clench, the scented pepper on his breath wafting to her nostrils.

She stands firm. Around them, guests enter the courtyard of the house. Many anticipate the coming of the prophet.

Devorah will not say what they both know—that she has never breathed a word about Simon's son approaching her on the street. Can the Pharisee not pay her this small kindness for dissuading his heir? Can he not allow her an insignificant corner of his home?

After a long while, Simon releases a sigh. "Go. Do your best to hide yourself."

She nods in gratitude, moving into the courtyard and up the veranda steps. She finds the room where an empty U-shaped dining couch sits.

Devorah seeks the wall behind the middle of the table, where she knows Jesus will lie as the guest of honor. She kneels atop the baked clay tiles and tugs her headscarf to hide her face.

When the guests enter, she watches Jesus greet his host warmly. He leaves his cloak at the door so as to not make the home of a Pharisee unclean. Simon gives a kiss of greeting to each guest.

All except one.

The servants bring water and olive oil to each guest.

All except one.

Heat rises in Devorah's chest. Simon did not invite this prophet to his home to honor him, he invited him to shame him! To confront him, perhaps, in front of his distinguished guests. Such a disgrace! How can the blessing over the meal be offered without each guest washing their hands and feet and dabbing them with oil? Even she, a common prostitute, clings to this sacred ritual.

Devorah's hands tremble as Jesus reclines among the cushions with the others at the table. She wants him to stand up and refuse to dine at Simon's home. She wants him to call out Simon's inhospitality.

But he does not. He simply smiles at the other guests and bows his head as Simon recites the blessing.

Rivulets of silent tears course down Devorah's cheeks. She thought to anoint Jesus's hand or head with a small amount of oil after he eats, but now what? Simon has shamed him.

Her tears pour forth, giving her an idea. In a bold move, she pulls out the alabaster jar at her neck. If Simon refuses the guest of honor the normal rituals of respect, she will perform them herself. These people already think poorly of her. What does it matter? She only cares what one person in this room thinks.

To climb upon the couch to wash his hands and anoint his head would not do, but his feet are in front of her as he reclines. Unclean feet are not a private matter.

She shimmies toward Jesus's feet, her tears flowing as she thinks of all this man has granted her. Freedom from her past, a new future, a bridge between her and Adonai. Her sobs come freely now, echoing through the room.

She cares not.

She lowers her head, allowing plentiful tears to fall upon his dirtied, calloused feet. Shame is cast upon her in this room, but she counts it as nothing if it means sharing in this man's humiliation. She knows the Shekinah of HaShem resides in this man, and so she will cling to him alone.

Jesus's body turns at her touch. She moves her headscarf aside and dries her feet with the only thing worthy of him—her hair.

Only a husband is meant to see a bride's hair. And although many men have indeed seen her long brown locks, this is the last man she will give herself to—not in a fleeting, physical way, but with her entire heart. From now on, she vows loyalty to him alone.

Gasps fill the room, but she is undeterred. Great love spurs great sacrifice.

As she works, awkward silence swallows the room. Doubt consumes her. Will Jesus accept her reverent gesture? Does he understand all he has done for her?

She lowers her head to kiss his feet and then unstops her alabaster flask, pouring the entirety of her expensive perfume on his skin. The scent of roses and irises fill the air. She can practically feel Simon's silent condemnations. No doubt, he is thinking that if Jesus were truly a prophet, he would know what kind of woman touches him.

She massages one last drop of oil into his feet and then covers her hair, sliding away to let the rabbi resume his dinner.

But instead, Jesus speaks. "Simon, I have something to tell you."

Devorah swallows. Will Jesus apologize on her behalf? Will he reject her?

"Tell me, teacher." Simon's tone pretends courtesy.

"Two people owed money to a certain moneylender. One owed him five hundred denarii, and the other fifty. Neither of them had the money to pay him back, so he forgave the debts of both."

Devorah listens intently.

"Now," Jesus says. "Which of them will love him more?"

Simon glances at her. "I suppose the one who had the bigger debt forgiven."

"You have judged correctly." Jesus turns toward Devorah, but still addresses Simon. "Do you see this woman? I came into your house. You did not give me any water for my feet, but she wet my feet with her tears and wiped them with her hair. You did not give me a kiss, but this woman, from the time I entered, has not stopped kissing my feet. You did not put oil on my head, but she has poured perfume on my feet. Therefore, I tell you, her many sins have been forgiven—as her great love has shown."

Devorah's heart overflows. The teacher has not rejected her or apologized for her—he is *defending* her in front of the Pharisee.

"But whoever has been forgiven little loves little." Jesus meets her gaze. "Your faith has saved you; go in peace."

She bows low to kiss his feet one last time, peace indeed running through her and over her and around her.

Peace, rest, and forgiveness in this life and the one to come.

Reflection Questions

The woman's great love and action are motivated by the fact that she has been forgiven and loved. Meditate on how these truths move in your own life.

Reflect on the parts of this woman's faith. She has accepted Jesus's words with her mind, stepped into a daily walk of trust, and responded in action. What parts of this faith do you struggle with? What parts do you tend to lean into?

Prayer

Gracious Father, thank you for your vast, nearly inconceivable love. You know the spaces and corners of our hearts. You know our deepest sins and our most shameful secrets and yet still beckon us to you. Help us move about in life beneath your grace, pouring forth love and gratitude. Amen.

Suggested Reading

Luke 7:36–50

Philippians 3:7–14

FOURTEEN

Unseen Child

Inspired by Mark 10:13–16

For days, she has waited to see him. And now that she is this close . . .

Abigail swipes a small, dirtied finger beneath her eyelid. She will not cry. Father does not approve of tears, and the teacher certainly will not either, if he happens to glimpse her sulky eyes through the crowd.

One of the teacher's followers—a large man with a gruff voice—sweeps his hand through the air. "You must take your children home. The teacher is tired and busy with healing."

If she were sick, would she have a better chance of seeing the teacher? But she is not sick. At least, not that anyone can tell. Her hurt scrapes her insides, not her outsides.

With bowed heads and disappointed frowns, parents nudge their children away from the teacher. Some of the mothers hold the hands of their little ones, and she tries not to stare at the connection of fingers and palms. She should go home. Trek back through the wild capers and mustard and dandelions. Her father and her uncles will be home from the market where they sell their perfumes. Her aunts will need help preparing food.

The thought sends her pressing forward, against the crowd. She's come too far on her own, and yet when she woke this morning, she could think of nothing else. As if a melody more beautiful than King David's harp called her to the mountainside.

"Don't stop the little children from coming to me." The voice cuts through the hum of the crowd, pulls her closer.

Some of the crowd turns back in his direction, and she trips over the foot of a large man.

"Watch it!" The man sneers down at her. She ducks beneath the garments of women and men and children until she reaches the place where Jesus entertains a dozen children.

But they all have parents looking on. Mothers who have sought the teacher's blessing for their sons. For their daughters.

She is alone.

She remembers her mother's face. She tries to push it away lest it make her cry again, but it clings to the corners of her memory. She was so pale and thin as she lay on her threadbare pallet, the fever eating away at her body. Abigail recalls the feel of her mother's weak fingers trailing over her face.

"Be a good girl for your aunts, dear child. My Abigail. Cling to Adonai. Let him comfort you after I am gone."

She begged her mother not to go to their ancestors, not to leave her alone with her aunts who busily tend their own children, with her father whom she only sees during the family's daily Torah readings.

But it was no use. Her mother left. And Abigail has been alone ever since.

The voice tugs her from her memories. Crisp and clear, like a cool breeze on a hot day. "Let the children come to me. Don't stop them! For the kingdom of heaven belongs to those who are like these children."

She peers around a small boy and finally sees him.

A wedge of disappointment pricks her spirit. He is ordinary, much like the men she sees at the market and at the synagogue, with dark hair, dark eyes, a slightly aquiline nose. Yet she supposes he is not horrible to look at. Who is she to judge, anyway? Aunt Maya tells Abigail that her eyes are too small for her head.

In the next moment, she forgets what her aunt says, for the teacher's gaze lands on her. In a twinkling as quick as the vivid blue streaks of lightning that sometimes brighten the night sky, her opinion of his ordinariness changes. For in those deep eyes, her soul unwraps.

He holds his hand out. "Abigail. Come, child."

She cranes her neck to look behind her. Surely, he speaks to another? But she does not see another girl, and when she dares to meet his soft gaze again, he nods, extending his hand farther.

The other children allow her through. Hesitant, she walks forward. Perhaps he wants to ask her about her older cousin, Jared. Jared has memorized the entire Torah and will train under Rabbi Abrams in the fall.

Yes, that is it. The teacher wants Jared, a boy who has been fattened with the Torah as an ox is fattened in the stall. The rabbi has no interest in her, a waif of a girl who becomes especially fidgety when the Sabbath lamp is lit.

She stands before him, knees quivering.

"Child," he says. "Abigail." As if she is the only one in this crowd.

She lifts her eyes to his and finds only warmth and understanding.

"Your mother's soul is well. You are not alone. I see you."

Her mouth falls open. Aunt Tabitha would admonish her to shut it lest she catch flies, but she cannot. How does he know about her mother? How does he know the words she longs to hear?

You are not alone.

As if she is enough, just as she is. Weak as she is.

He lays a hand on her head and speaks a blessing over her. She cannot focus on his words but realizes the impact upon her spirit.

The teacher sees her. His message is from Adonai. Something unexplainable tells her *he* is from Adonai. And with this knowing, her spirit finds peace.

When she goes home, nothing will be changed. But because of her encounter with the teacher, *she* will be changed. And that is enough.

Reflection Questions

Why do you think Jesus put so much emphasis on loving not only the children but the poor and downtrodden? What does this tell us about the character of God?

When have you been tempted to shove away someone who simply needed to be recognized, acknowledged? When was a time you felt misunderstood and alone?

Prayer

Father, comfort us this day. Help us seek you as if we were a child in this crowd. Give us a tender heart for the hurting.

Give us wisdom in the trying places in our lives. May your grace transform our perspectives when it comes to difficult people and difficult circumstances. Father, help us depend on your presence in every minute of this day. Amen.

Suggested Reading

Matthew 19:13–30

Mark 10:13–16

FIFTEEN

Wife of a Manager

Inspired by Luke 8:1–3

She runs her fingers over the carnelian necklace Chuza gifted her on the night of their wedding. He'd been attentive and gentle that night. The feel of the smooth crystals beneath her touch conjures a fondness for her husband she has tried to push aside for weeks.

Feelings of attachment will not aid her in what she must do.

She places the necklace in the trunk alongside her entire collection of jewels and silks. Her looking brass and coins and gold combs. Ribbons, bone bracelets, lapis beads. She prays Jesus will find it all helpful in supporting him and his disciples. She prays he will not deny her in joining their company.

She closes the trunk.

"Joanna?"

She startles at her husband's voice. "Chuza. I-I thought you were with the king."

The tetrarch, more accurately.

Her husband's gaze falls on the trunk. The corners of his mouth turn downward. "You did not tell me you scheduled a trip."

She swallows. Chuza usually allows her to come and go as she wishes. Though she used to serve Phasaelis, Antipas's first wife, her friend fled the palace after the king took up with his brother's wife, Herodias. Herodias had scorned Joanna's services, likely sensing her loyalty to her former mistress.

"I must go see him again." The boldness in her voice belies the trembling within.

Chuza's handsome face furrows, making him look older than his forty years. "The rabbi from Nazareth."

"Yes. Jesus."

"But he has healed you. What more do you need of him?"

To be with him, she thinks, but she cannot say the words. Chuza will form false notions, and unlike her husband, she has been faithful in their marriage.

"I wish to aid his ministry."

"Joanna, that is impossible. I do not wish my wife to run around with such rabble."

"The king is curious about Jesus—you said so yourself."

"All the more reason for you to stay away," he snaps. "If your rabbi ends up like the Baptist, you need not be associated with him."

John. First, their son, then the loss of her only friend, Phasaelis, and then John. True, she did not know the Immerser well, but that one visit into the dank prison cell was enough to give her hope. It was enough to cause her to run to Jesus.

She looks out the window onto the courtyard of the fortress, the very place where Salome had danced for Antipas and his guests on the king's birthday. The king had not wanted to kill

John, but Herodias's daughter's request couldn't be denied—not in front of such esteemed company, the emperor's advisers chief among them.

The king would stop at no ends to curry favor with Tiberias, even building his ostentatious new palace in a town named after the emperor.

"I cannot go to Tiberias. If I'm forced to live upon the graves of my people, the evil spirits will take hold again." She does not lie. The city, nestled on the Sea of Galilee, is said to be built on the burial grounds of the Hebrew people. The entirety of it is unclean. How can she live and worship in such a place? Then again, how has she lived and worshiped in Antipas's palace all these years?

She had not understood a better way. But now, with Jesus . . .

"Are the rabbi's spells so weak that you will succumb to the spirits again at a change in location?" He pulls her close, tucks her head in the crook of his neck. "My darling, I cannot bear to live without you."

She closes her eyes against the familiar smell of him—spikenard and cinnamon. They have been through much since he first gifted her the necklace tucked in her trunk. A painful and adulterous affair on his part and then forgiveness on her part, only for their relationship to be tested by the death of their eleven-year-old son nine months ago and the demons that had overtaken her soon after.

Only her visit to Jesus had given her hope, had made her want to live again.

But not for the purpose of gathering fine things and eating sumptuous food or reveling in her husband's esteemed position as the king's manager. None of that mattered any longer.

Only the things of HaShem mattered now, only the kingdom John spoke of, the kingdom Jesus ushers in.

She grips Chuza's hand. "Come with me."

Chuza pushes her away and laughs, a nervous edge fraying the sound. "And leave the king? Have you gone mad?"

Any affection between them is leached from the extravagant room. She stares at the cypress planks of the floor. "It is not preposterous. Many follow him."

Her husband lowers his voice. "Even if I took leave of my senses and agreed, the king would not have it. I would be next on the chopping block."

Though she thinks Chuza inflates his worth to the tetrarch, she knows Antipas would not take kindly to his manager leaving his service to follow an itinerant rabbi.

"Please, do not make me go to Tiberias," she whispers. "I cannot do it."

"You expect me to give you my blessing to chase after another man—to sleep among his tents and supply for his needs with money the king granted us while in his services? What kind of a man allows women to trail after him as if they are part of his harem, anyway? What kind of a man would I be to allow my wife to do so?"

Her face heats. "It is not as you make it sound. He is a man of Adonai, Chuza. Without him, I would be wasting away in bed, haunted." She shivers, remembering the absolute despair that swallowed her days after their son died. She'd wanted to die. One desperate night, she'd found herself in the prison below the Machaerus fortress, begging the guards to run a sword through her.

That's when she'd met John.

"Will you not allow me to do this, at least for the season?"

Since Jesus healed her, she can think of nothing but following him, giving what she has to his purpose and his kingdom.

Chuza looks out the window into the courtyard. Potted ferns wave in the breeze, reminding Joanna of the wave offerings made at the temple. Both she and Chuza have neglected the things of HaShem for too long. They allowed themselves to become enamored with the things of Rome, the things of the Herodians, the things of the world.

No longer.

Finally, he sighs. "I will miss you." He reaches for her and kisses the top of her head with cold lips.

She flings her arms around him, her heart growing wings and even newfound fondness for her husband. "Thank you, Chuza. Thank you. I will be back, I promise."

Her husband straightens. "I must go to the king." His gaze drops to her trunk. "Shalom, my wife."

"Shalom, Chuza."

And then he is gone, leaving Joanna to take in the colorful pillows and ornamental rugs of the room one last time. She will miss none of it, for what Jesus offers is of much greater value.

Reflection Questions

Read Luke 8:1–3. What circumstances do you imagine propelled Joanna to make such a remarkable change in her life? Who are some people you know (in either the present or the past) who made a drastic change to follow Jesus?

Both John the Baptist and Jesus spoke against Herod Antipas. In both John's death and Jesus's execution, Herod plays the part of an indecisive ruler, carried along by the whims of those around him. In what ways can being indecisive hinder the things of God? Alternately, when is it prudent to take time to think and pray for wisdom?

Prayer

Heavenly Father, help us follow you with an undivided heart. Give us wisdom to make hard decisions, to choose not just what is good but what is best. Give us grace to love those around us. Father, thank you for seeking after each of us, your sheep. Amen.

Suggested Reading

Luke 8:1–3

Luke 24:1–12

SIXTEEN

A Legion of Blessing

Inspired by Mark 5:1–20

He belongs with the dead.

That is what the demons tell him.

Once in a while, memory of a different life teases the fringes of his mind, but it never solidifies. He can no longer discern what is real and what is imagined.

It has been too long. He is not separate from them—he is *them.*

He moans, pushing away from the limestone cavern with stilted, harried movements. His bare skin is wet, but he does not remember a storm. He squats at a mess of pointed stones, soiling what little is left of his flax tunic. The scent of urine rises to meet him, and he succumbs to the familiar black haze of his mind.

You are death.

You are alone.

You are nothing.

Even your own mother rejected you.

Succumb to us.

Be like us.

There is no hope.

He whimpers again, grabs for a pointed shard of rock. It is familiar and comforting in his hand, and he slashes the inside of his arm. The pain stings, the ooze of blood flows warm, then burns. His mind cannot comprehend much, but it comprehends pain. In the discomfort, he knows part of himself is still alive. Part of himself is still human.

Voices of men come to him from across the lake. Why are they here? Have they come to bury their dead?

He stumbles toward the sea but throws himself down after a few steps, convulsing on the sharp rocks.

He wants to go to them.

He wants to stay hidden. The swine are not far. He should stay with them.

Go.

Or stay.

He crawls toward the lake, each movement slow, the voices both straining and compelling. As he draws closer, he senses something from his old life. Something not black and hopeless.

He screams, pushing himself onto his feet. He sees the men now. One calls to him. He falls forward in halting, running steps.

The man calls again, but as he comes closer, fear grips him. He knows this man. He knows what he can do to him. He *has* come for them.

He moans, falling at his feet.

The man speaks. "Come out of this man, you impure spirit!"

His body shudders with the recognition that accompanies the voice. "What do you want with me, Jesus, Son of the Most

High God? In God's name don't torture me!" He screams the words, his voice echoing off the glassy lake.

A hand touches his bare shoulder. He jerks away at the foreign sensation of human contact.

"What is your name?"

"My name is Legion, for we are many. Please, do not send us out of the area." He grasps Jesus's ankles. "Send us among the pigs. Allow us to go into them."

He tastes sand and silt. He clings. He begs, for what, he does not know. The demons beg. He begs. They are one.

"Go."

The one word draws the blackness from him. Like a spool of fishing line coming undone, the one word sets off a release within him.

His mind clears.

All is quiet.

He blinks.

It is so . . . still.

Above and behind him come sounds of swine grunting and running. Then the immense splash of something falling from great heights into the water.

He raises his head, daring to meet Jesus's gaze. "They are gone?"

One corner of Jesus's mouth tilts. "They are gone. Get up. Bathe in the lake. Peter here has an extra tunic."

The man obeys, his thoughts righting as he slides beneath the green jade of the lake and comes up renewed. He takes in the vivid rusty ocher of the cliffs reflecting on the water. How has he not comprehended their beauty before now? There is much to remember. But all of it seems secondary to the overwhelming need to find out more about this Jesus. The demons testified who he was—were they lying about that too?

After he bathes, he joins the men by a fire on the beach. They cook fish. His mouth waters. They offer him food. He chews carefully, slowly.

It is good.

It is so good!

He listens as Jesus teaches them how to pray. He teaches them about letting light shine on a stand, about giving enemies good things.

Everything he says seems overturned. And yet at the same time, it is right. This world is right.

"Perhaps you can tell us your true name now?" Jesus asks after his teaching.

"I am Aron."

Mountain of Strength—that is what his mother used to tell him. Now, because of Jesus, perhaps it can be true.

The next morning, people from the town and countryside come to see him. When they see Aron in his right mind, they beg Jesus to leave. Aron pleads with them, but there is no dissuading the crowd. Why do they want this man, who has done so much for him, to leave? What are they afraid of?

Soon after, though, the disciples prepare for their trip back to Capernaum.

Again, Aron falls at Jesus's feet. "Please, let me go with you!" How will he survive without this man, this Son of the Most High? How can he be at peace, how can he be safe, if not in his presence?

"Aron, return home to your own people. Tell them how much the Lord has done for you, and how he has had mercy on you."

"Lord, when will I see you again?"

"I have a feeling it will be soon." There is a knowing in his eyes.

Aron nods. While he does not wish to leave Jesus, he is anxious to see his father and mother, to tell them what God has done. He will tell his friends, his neighbors—everyone in the Decapolis! They saw how hopeless he was, but no longer.

He has found Hope himself.

Reflection Questions

The demons lied to Aron about who he was. What lies have you believed about who you are? What truths about your identity in Christ can you remind yourself of to safeguard against such lies?

Imagine this man's joyful reunion with his family. What do you think he first said to them?

Prayer

Most High God, you are Lord over the angels and the demons, over life and death, over hardship and danger, over the present and the future. Thank you for the enormous height and length and depth of your love. Amen.

Suggested Reading

Mark 5:1–20

Luke 8:26–39

SEVENTEEN

Forever Unclean

Inspired by Mark 5:21-43

It is desperation that pushes her toward him.

Desperation, and a fragile sliver of hope.

It is not hard to follow. The crowd ushers Talia along as if in the swift current of a stream. Black spots flicker before her eyes. Will she faint? She is weak—always weak. What would it be like to wake with energy, to run as she once had as a little girl? To have enough strength to swim in the Galilean Sea?

She remembers how the hazzan fell at Jesus's feet moments earlier, how he begged the teacher from Nazareth to come lay his hands on his dying daughter, to heal her. His heartfelt request caused a thread of longing to pull within her, unspooling deep sadness. If only she had a father or a husband who would approach the teacher as this man does on behalf of his daughter.

But she has no one. Even her friends have long grown weary of her plight, her neediness, her uncleanliness, her preoccupation with finding a cure. She has tried a myriad of concoctions—purple aloes, curdled milk, maidenhair fern, even barleycorn found in the dung of a white mule. She has allowed doctors to bleed her. She has sought prayers and sacrificed many animals.

Nothing has helped. She has been bleeding for twelve long years.

Just as she is certain the black spots will consume her, that she will pass out and be trampled by the crowd, she catches sight of the rabbi's familiar head through the mass of people. Just the sight of him stirs up fierce, desperate determination.

She will not faint now.

If she can just draw near enough to touch the wings of his garments, she *will* be healed, she knows it.

Just the fringe of his clothes.

With the dregs of her strength, she pushes forward. The black spots come but she forces air into her nostrils and prays a wordless, unspoken plea that she will reach him. He does not have to know. And if his power should curse her as the power of the ark of the covenant killed Uzzah, then at least she tried. At least she did what she could do.

Tears burn her eyes with the effort. She reaches out a hand, no longer mindful of whom she touches. Nothing matters but getting to him.

Her fingers strain, his mantle just out of reach. Should she lunge forward, risk the descent of her body on the packed dirt? Before she can decide, however, someone shoves her from behind and she falls, hand outstretched. Black spots. A rough mantle. Blue and white tassels. Falling . . . falling . . .

The tips of her fingers brush the tzitzit on the wings of his garment just before she hits the ground. She anticipates the impact of the hard dirt, but she does not feel it. Time stands still. Something new swirls within her, exchanging brokenness and pain with health and vitality.

Talia sits up, places her hand over her womb. The ache is gone. She does not feel the flow. The black spots have disappeared. In their place, she sees more clearly than ever. Strength courses through her limbs.

She is free.

The teacher stops walking, but his disciples continue forward, shouting at the crowd to make way.

"Who touched my clothes?"

Was this it, then? The moment HaShem will strike her down like Uzzah because she dared take what was not hers?

The teacher turns and asks again, this time louder. "Who touched my clothes?"

One of the rabbi's followers—an intimidating man with a demeanor a Roman soldier might not even toy with—looks at Jesus, exasperation upon his ruddy face. He gestures to the massive throng. "Rabbi, you see the people crowding against you and yet you can ask, 'Who touched me?'"

But the teacher ignores him and searches the crowd. "Someone touched me; I know that power has gone out from me."

Though her legs feel stronger than they have in years, they tremble as she comes forward, falling at his feet much as the hazzan had. She cannot look at him. She simply presses her face to the dirt at his sandals.

"Forgive me, teacher. Forgive me." Her body shakes. "I knew if I touched you, I would be healed." Slowly, she raises her gaze to his dark eyes. They surprise her with their softness, and the tension in her body drains away. "And I am healed. I have been sick twelve years, and I am healed."

One corner of his mouth lifts and he touches her shoulder. *Touches* her.

"Daughter," he says. "Your faith has healed you. Go in peace and be freed from your suffering."

She will ponder the words forever. She tucks them away to store in her mind and take out to contemplate and caress like a smooth river stone. She says them over and over again to herself as Jesus's attention turns to the hazzan, and Talia departs from the crowd and runs—yes, runs!—to the sea.

Your faith has healed you.

Go in peace.

Be freed from suffering.

But most important is what he has called her. The identity she now claims.

Daughter.

Reflection Questions

Jesus remarks that the woman's "faith has healed" her. Where did the woman place her faith? How does her action back up this faith?

How might Jesus calling the woman "daughter" serve to heal her in a way that goes beyond the physical? What does the fact that Jesus heals this ostracized woman before he heals the daughter of a well-respected synagogue ruler say about his upside-down kingdom?

Prayer

Lord, thank you for being our beautiful Savior, our heavenly Father, our ultimate Healer. May we reach out our hands to touch you—not only for deliverance but to draw nearer to you in your splendor and grace. May we turn to those around us with the same intentional attention you gave this woman. Amen.

Suggested Reading

Mark 5:21–43
Matthew 9:18–26
Luke 8:40–56

EIGHTEEN

A Sick Daughter

Inspired by Mark 5:21-43

He should have come sooner.

The single thought consumes Jairus as he realizes Jesus is no longer following him. Why has he stopped?

He thinks of his little Adi, home in bed. The rattling in her throat shook him to the core, compelling him to finally seek out the rabbi who often taught in the synagogue. Jairus thinks of his wife, shriveled with grief, already mourning their daughter who is still alive.

She is still alive. There *is* hope!

But for how long?

Jairus pushes through the disciples to see why Jesus has stopped following him. A woman in worn clothing cowers at his feet, confessing to touching the teacher.

What is so important that she must stop Jesus from coming to his daughter? Is this woman's child sick? Can she not wait until later?

But then Jesus speaks. "Daughter," he says. "Your faith has healed you. Go in peace and be freed from your suffering."

And something withers within him. In Jesus's words to the woman, he glimpses the only thing that he, a loving father, cannot provide for his own daughter.

Healing. Life. Complete care.

Even though he is one of the most respected men in town, even though he has gone up to Yerushalayim many times over the course of Adi's young life to offer sacrifices for her healing, it is not enough.

It has never been enough.

But here, in Jesus's words to this bedraggled woman, Jairus glimpses a fullness—a fulfillment, even.

"Master." Jairus turns to see the drawn and tired face of his household servant. "You need not bother the teacher anymore. I am sorry, master. Your daughter is dead."

At first, he does not believe the words. How can they be true—his little Adi, who loved to lay on the roof and count the stars, who used to greet him when he returned from the synagogue by searching his pockets for pistachios he'd picked up from the market on the way home?

But then the words sink in. His chest twists.

No . . . no, it cannot be.

Jesus comes beside him, somehow exuding a nonsensical peace that wars with the pain clawing at Jairus's innards. "Do not be afraid, Jairus. Just believe."

Believe? Believe in what? His daughter is dead—what is left? But then he remembers the words Jesus spoke to the woman. The rabbi does not seem to require much besides faith.

Jesus beckons three of his disciples to continue with them. The rest keep the crowd at bay. In minutes, they reach Jairus's comfortable neighborhood. His home contains a crowd, the courtyard bursting with flutists and mourners, wailing and crying. Howling shrieks vibrate through him, tempting him to succumb to grief, to tear his robes and pour ashes on his head.

But Jesus said not to be afraid. To believe. Jairus recognizes only a few family members as true mourners. How have they all arrived so quickly? Did they know he departed to get the teacher? Did they hope to see a healing and, now that all was lost, turn their curiosity to mourning?

He leads Jesus into the courtyard.

"Why all this commotion and wailing?" Jesus asks. "The child is not dead, but asleep."

The howls diminish. Those in the crowd look to one another. But then a mouth twitches, a nervous giggle comes.

It is more than Jairus can bear. All he wants is to get to his daughter and wife. "Out," he demands, and Jesus, Peter, James, and John usher the crowd from the house.

At last, there is silence. Mariamne stands outside Adi's bedchamber. Jairus wraps his arms around his wife's quaking body.

"Jairus," Jesus says. "May we see the child?"

Jairus squeezes his wife's hand and nods before leading the men into Adi's room.

Do not be afraid.

Just believe.

His little Adi is still in her bed. Her struggle for breath has ceased, the furrow in her brow smoothed. There is no more life.

Jairus begs Jesus with his eyes. He does believe! That his faith may work wonders as it did for that woman in the street! That his faith may be enough for his daughter—and where it is not enough, that the teacher may fill it in, like wine fills a wineskin.

He believes!

Jesus reaches for Adi's hand, unflinching as his skin touches the child's corpse.

"Talitha koum!" he says with firm authority.

Little girl, I say to you, get up!

When Adi blinks and opens her eyes, Jairus gasps, emotion clamping down on his throat. Mariamne clutches his arm.

Slowly, Adi props herself up on her elbows, glances at her parents, then meets Jesus's gaze. "Are you a doctor?"

Jesus smiles. "Sometimes, I am a doctor."

She shimmies to a sitting position. "You are a good doctor. I feel very well."

Jairus and Mariamne crush her to themselves, laughing, sobbing, uttering praises to Adonai.

Jairus tears away all too soon to fall at Jesus's feet. "Master, you have provided what I, her father, could not. Thank you."

"You are welcome." He looks at the three disciples standing agape. "We must not tell anyone about this."

They all nod, including Jairus.

"I think it best to get your daughter something to eat, Jairus. I have a feeling she is hungry."

Reflection Questions

Why do you think it was important that the mourners leave before Jesus performed his miracle?

Meditate on Jesus's words: *Do not be afraid. Just believe.* How do these words strike you? Do you find them difficult at all? In what way might they comfort you?

Prayer

Perfect heavenly Father, thank you for being a God of fulfillment, a God of completeness and unity. When we struggle to make sense of our suffering and the suffering in this world, help us hear your voice saying, "Do not be afraid. Just believe." Help us rest, Lord, in you. Amen.

Suggested Reading

Mark 5: 21–43

Matthew 9:18–26

Luke 8:40–56

NINETEEN

Overcoming Unbelief

Inspired by Mark 9:14–29

Ephraim holds his breath as the man named Philip anoints his son with oil. At fourteen, Simon stands a head shorter than Ephraim and stares at the ground, waiting. The boy is not a stranger to healers and physicians. Ephraim's departed wife scraped all of Galilee for help, to no avail.

Philip stands over Simon and throws back his shoulders as he casts a hand toward the boy. "I command you, come out of him!"

The crowd silences. Ephraim releases his breath. They have tried so many times. Could this moment be their salvation?

He glances at the nine disciples, followers of Jesus of Nazareth. Ephraim sought out the teacher in hopes of helping his son, but the rabbi was not with his disciples. Yet the men assured Ephraim they could perform a healing. Perhaps the man named Philip would cure Simon this very minute.

"Did it work?" One of the teachers of the law asks from where he stands at the edge of the crowd.

"Of course it worked," the disciple says. "I performed a similar healing in Sepphoris last season."

Ephraim places his hands on his son's shoulders. When the demon attacks, Simon's eyes grow cloudy. Now, they look clear. "How do you feel, Simon?"

Could this be it? True healing for his son? The birth of a new kind of life for them? Now that his wife is gone, he is helpless to watch over both the shop and Simon, exhausted from guarding the fire so the demon will not throw his son upon the flames.

"How do you feel?" Ephraim asks again. If Simon is healed, surely he will speak again as he had during childhood.

He studies him. But the familiar haze overtakes his son's eyes. Dark desperation works beneath his own breastbone. "Come, son." He guides Simon to lay on the ground. The damage will be lessened if they deprive the demon of the opportunity to hurl him to the earth.

When it comes, he watches helplessly as his son's body shakes, his eyes roll back in his head, his teeth gnash, and a foamy white froth trails from his mouth onto the dirt. He places a hand on Simon's arm. It is all he can do. If within this tortured body there is a part of his boy that is Simon, Ephraim prays he will register his father's touch. He prays Simon knows his father will not abandon him, no matter what.

One of the teachers of the law begins to argue with Philip. "You did not anoint him properly or say the correct invocation."

"If you think you can do better, I invite you to try," the disciple says.

Ephraim wants to weep. He wants to take his son home so they can be away from the arguing and the curious gazes.

He waits for the demon to release its hold, and his son slowly ceases shaking. Taking a piece of flax cloth, Ephraim wipes Simon's mouth and helps him stand.

"It's our rabbi!" Another disciple points in the direction of Mount Tabor, where four men walk toward them. The bickering group moves to greet them. Ephraim follows, leading Simon by the hand. A glow lights the men's faces. Have they been in the presence of angels? Or perhaps they have simply been in the sun too long.

"What are you arguing about?" the man in the front asks the disciples.

So, this is Jesus. Ephraim stomps out the wedge of hope within him before it can gain a foothold.

Still, what does he have to lose?

He pushes forward and kneels before the rabbi. "Teacher, I brought you my son, who is possessed by a spirit that has robbed him of speech." Ephraim lifts his head to search the man's eyes. "Whenever it seizes him, it throws him to the ground. He foams at the mouth, gnashes his teeth and becomes rigid. I asked your disciples to drive out the spirit, but they could not."

Jesus glances at the nine men, his mouth firm. "You unbelieving generation. How long shall I stay with you? How long shall I put up with you? Bring the boy to me."

Ephraim turns and searches the crowd for Simon, who stands before a teacher of the law. The scribe utters an invocation over him. Ephraim grabs his son. "Come, Simon."

But as soon as his son is in sight of the rabbi, the demon throws him to the dirt. His body thrashes. White lather dribbles from his mouth. Ephraim kneels beside Simon, and Jesus lowers himself also, studying the boy.

"How long has he been like this?"

"From childhood. It has often thrown him into the fire or water to kill him. I am a metalsmith. It is difficult to do my work and protect my son from the fires. But if you can do anything, take pity on us and help us."

Jesus raises an eyebrow. "'If you can'?"

Ephraim bites his lip, remembering Jesus's words from moments before about bearing with the unbelief of his disciples. He has *tried* to believe. Over and over again. First in the healers and then in the priests and then in the doctors and then in this man's disciples.

How can one cling to belief when there are so many reasons *not* to believe? And how can one summon up the strength to make oneself believe?

But he *is* here, seeking out this man. Is that not a step of faith, however small?

He resists the urge to tear his tunic. Jesus is right here. But what if Ephraim hinders his son's healing with his unbelief? What if he is why Simon can't be made well?

"Everything is possible for one who believes," Jesus says.

Ephraim groans, a deep uttering that mirrors the struggle within his soul. "I do believe; help me overcome my unbelief!"

The teacher stands. "You deaf and mute spirit, I command you, come out of him and never enter him again."

Simon shrieks—a sound so frightening and foreign that Ephraim stands frozen. His son shakes more violently than ever, the demon battering him about on the ground. Ephraim is nearly throttled by an arm. Finally, his body stills.

Simon's pale face no longer contorts. Is he . . . alive?

Jesus touches him. Simon's eyes open, clear and seeing. The rabbi helps the boy to his feet.

Simon's gaze lands on Ephraim. "Abba?"

Ephraim gasps. "Yes, yes, my son. It is I!"

"It is gone, Abba."

Ephraim nods, eyes filling with tears. "I know." He falls at Jesus's feet. "Thank you, teacher. Thank you for granting this for us."

Ephraim could not provide what his son needed. He could not even provide belief for his healing.

This man Jesus had done all of it, and more.

Reflection Questions

The father's statement in Mark 9:24 indicates there is a measure of belief, as he is calling to Jesus for help. Yet in a profound and humble moment, he also recognizes his belief is not complete or perfect or enough. How does his statement relate to the parable of the mustard seed in Matthew 13:31–32?

After the demon leaves the boy, many believe him dead, but Jesus doesn't allow the boy to succumb to either demons or death. "Jesus took him by the hand and lifted him to his feet." How does this part of the story resonate with you?

Prayer

Heavenly Father, thank you that you measure belief by seeds rather than tall trees. When we are tempted to look to ourselves or even our great faith, may you remind us that we need look only to you. Lord, we do believe—help us overcome our unbelief! Amen.

Suggested Reading

Mark 9:2–29

Matthew 17:14–21

Luke 9:37–43

TWENTY

More Than Bread

Inspired by Mark 6:30–44 and John 6:1–15

Josiah's stomach rumbles as he watches his aunt place two pickled fish wrapped in a strip of flax in his basket alongside five small loaves of barley bread. Though he is sick of the crumbly barley, it is better than the alternative—nothing.

His aunt hands him the small basket. "It is all I have for you, Josiah. There will be many pilgrims on the road up to Yerushalayim. The kindhearted will share."

He nods and hugs her withered frame. She has been thick in grief since hearing of John the Immerser's death at the hands of Herod Antipas. Josiah still cannot believe the man who guided him beneath the Jordan River last year is no longer alive.

He is twelve—nearly a man, yet he does not know how to comfort his aunt. And now, the green fruit is on the fig tree and the month of Nisan has arrived. He must leave for the Holy City to celebrate the Feast of Passover.

He bids his aunt farewell, joining other travelers as they round the Sea of Galilee to travel through the Decapolis and Peraea. Many push carts piled high with the firstfruits of their harvests—barley, wheat, dates, pomegranates, figs, olives, and crowns of grapes—to be offered to Adonai.

He will finally be able to see the city of David and the temple, to participate in Passover in the most holy of ways.

"Josiah, come!" Some of his friends from Torah school call to him. They point to a boat just past the place where the Jordan enters the sapphire lake.

Josiah hesitates only a moment before joining his peers. "What is it?"

"The teacher from Nazareth is in the boat!" his friend Elias says.

Josiah's chest lurches. "The rabbi Jesus? He is here?" The Immerser baptized and blessed this man, even willing his disciples to leave him and follow after the other rabbi. But although Jesus spent much time in the neighboring town of Capernaum, Josiah has not yet seen the man.

"Some say he needs time away from the crowds, others that he is leaving Antipas's territory."

Bethsaida *is* just outside the dominion of the tetrarch who had killed the Baptist. Did the teacher plan to stay on this side of the lake?

"I am on my way to Yerushalayim." Should he continue to the Holy City or try to catch a glimpse of Jesus?

Elias points. His hair is plastered to his sweaty brow. "They are coming to shore!"

Josiah remembers the grief in his aunt's eyes and longs to bring her something of hope. Will Jesus speak to the crowds? Will he heal the impaired hobbling through the ford that leads from Capernaum?

As the boat comes to shore, Josiah cranes his neck to see the teacher, but there is nothing that marks him from the rest. Then, one of the men begins to speak to the crowd.

The rabbi's words are like a lamp, one that has been waiting to be lit for all Josiah's years. He speaks in parables—about a lost sheep and a lost son, about seed falling on good soil, about serving Adonai over money, about not worrying. The words reverberate inside Josiah, stirring to life a faith that began when the Immerser guided him beneath the Jordan.

After the teaching, Josiah sits with his schoolmates alongside a patch of myrrh blossoms. He watches as a man with a cane and a prominent limp makes his way to Jesus. A moment later, he is hugging Jesus, throwing down his cane, and *running* toward his family.

How is it possible? But Josiah knows. It is only possible with Adonai.

After performing more healings, the rabbi speaks to them again. Josiah's stomach rumbles but he refuses to eat the little food he has for his journey.

As evening approaches, the teacher stops speaking. Not long after, a tall, muscular disciple wanders the outskirts of the crowd. "Does anyone have anything to eat?"

Josiah swallows. Of course, the rabbi needs to eat. He has not asked for an offering, not even from those he has healed. He has been teaching and healing all day. They may all be hungry, but they have not all been doing the work of Jesus.

Do not worry about your life, what you will eat or drink . . . look at the birds of the air; they do not sow or reap or store away in barns, and yet your heavenly Father feeds them. Are you not much more valuable than they?

Josiah stands and pushes through the crowd toward the disciple, the handle of his food basket clutched in his fist.

"Sir, I have a small bit of food."

The man smiles, ruffles Josiah's hair, and peers into the basket, his face falling at the sight of the peasant lunch. Of course he is disappointed. Barley, after all, is grain given to animals and to the poor. The fish are no more than two bites. Should Josiah have stayed silent?

But the disciple beckons him. "Come. You may offer it to the teacher yourself."

Josiah follows the man. "Rabbi," the disciple calls. "Here is a boy with five small barley loaves and two small fish, but how far will they go among so many?"

The disciple ushers Josiah forward. With quivering hands, he offers the basket to Jesus. "I see you were listening to my words." Jesus places a hand on his shoulder. "Thank you for trusting me with your lunch, and with your journey to the Holy City."

Josiah blinks. How does Jesus know his destination?

"Have the people sit down," Jesus instructs his disciples. Josiah hears one of them worry aloud about a riot starting.

Jesus lifts one of the barley loaves. "Blessed are you, O Lord our God, King of the universe, who brings forth bread from the earth."

The disciples gather wicker baskets from among the crowd. When one comes by with a basket sometime later, it brims with barley bread.

The disciple gives Josiah seven small loaves—more than he had to begin with. Another comes with a basket of sardines. Even they seem surprised by the patience of the people, by the abundance of their master.

Josiah eats with his friends, and it is the most marvelous meal he has ever eaten. It is the abundance of food, yes, but it is more. It is the reminder of who provided it. It is the teaching still fresh in his mind. It is the community of those around him. It is the miracle of the bountiful meal, an obvious reminder of Moses and Elijah and Elisha, multiplying bread in the wilderness.

As darkness descends, the disciples distribute the leftovers to the needy and those on their way to Yerushalayim for Passover.

Josiah bids Elias goodbye. He stares at the ten loaves of bread and five fish he holds in his basket. More than enough. More than he started with.

He turns back home, intent on beginning his journey tomorrow. He must tell his aunt all that happened this day. He must restore the hope in her eyes with the words and deeds of the teacher John the Immerser prepared them for.

Reflection Questions

Jesus addresses not just the spiritual condition of the crowd but their physical condition—even giving an abundance of leftovers. What does this tell us about God?

Read John 6:47–51. How does the miraculous feeding of the thousands, this messianic banquet, point us toward the Holy Communion we can now participate in with one another?

Prayer

God Almighty, you have filled the hungry with good things—you have filled us with good things, both physical and spiritual. You have made us lie down in green pastures; you have filled our cups to overflowing. As we share your love with the world, help us remember your example. May we love with both our hands and our hearts. Amen.

Suggested Reading

Matthew 14:13–21
Mark 6:31–44
Luke 9:12–17
John 6:1–14

TWENTY-ONE

Weeping in Ramah

Inspired by Matthew 2:13–18

Hadara's hand trembles as she holds the flame to the yahrzeit candle. It has been thirty years, and still, this private memorial is never easy.

The candle sputters to life. It will burn for twenty-four hours. It is not much, but it is all she can do to remember Eitan, her only child, one of nineteen Bethlehem sons murdered by Herod thirty years ago.

She sits, staring at the flame. Her husband died fifteen years ago, leaving her in disgrace as a childless widow. She moved to Jericho to be near her sister, finding small solace in the willows and sweet calamus surrounding her new home.

Give me comfort, Adonai. I am not like Job—I am weak. I am bitter. I am old. And I will die without children.

For not only had Adonai allowed her small son to perish that long ago night but he had closed her womb as well.

She thinks of the firstborn sons Adonai spared in Egypt during the Passover, of the lambs' blood over the door that protected them. If she had known her son was in danger and if she had smeared lamb's blood along her doorpost, would he have been spared?

She shakes her head, forcing the question from her mind. It is no use, these could-have-beens. What's done is done.

Leaning back and closing her eyes, she remembers the weight of Eitan upon her chest. Her son was the oldest boy killed in Bethlehem that night, and he'd been starting to speak, many of the words mimics of her own. He'd been a beautiful child, with eyes so big and inquisitive they never missed anything. Her hands preparing bread, her husband throwing back his head when he laughed.

Hours before he died, she'd rocked him to sleep. "I love you, Eitan," she'd whispered.

Drowsily, he'd mumbled, "I love you, Ima."

Daniel had admonished her for rocking him to sleep when he was to be weaned in months. He didn't need his mother so much.

But she'd stood her ground, and now, she takes comfort in the fact that she made the most of every minute with her precious boy.

A tear slides down her cheek. Her only consolation is that she will someday die, and perhaps Adonai will allow her to see—to hold—her son again.

A knock sounds at her door, and she bites back a groan. It is past sunset. She is alone and defenseless, and although she often muses on the blessings of the afterlife, she is not certain it needs to be at the hands of a thief or murderer.

"Who is there?"

"A friend," the voice answers. "A friend in need."

She stands, her hand wavering at the door latch. She doesn't recognize the voice, and yet in a strange way it is familiar. Without thinking, she lifts the latch.

Before her stands a man of average stature. Her eyes adjust to the light, and she meets his gaze . . . those inquisitive eyes. Her breath catches. It can't be.

"Eitan?" Eitan . . . all grown up?

The man's mouth pulls downward. "I am not he." He studies her. His eyes shine beneath the light of Eitan's yahrzeit candle. "But I know him."

"You could not know him, for he died many years ago."

"I am sorry for his death."

"Why do you apologize?" she snaps. "Were you the man who wielded the sword?"

Why has he disturbed her peace on this night? She should never have opened the door.

A movement behind the man's cloak draws her attention. What does he hide?

"I was not, but I am the one for whom the sword was intended."

She blinks, studying him, attempting to piece his words together. Rumor had it Herod had been trying to kill a king that night. This man does not look like a king.

"I am sorry for your loss, Hadara."

She squints at him, somehow unsurprised he knows her name. Is he an angel sent by God?

She sniffs. "What are you hiding?"

The man turns and ushers forth a boy of about six. His face is tear-streaked and dirty. He clings to the man's tunic.

"My disciples brought him to me. His mother died many years ago and his father was killed by bandits yesterday. He has no kin."

Her heart softens at the sight of the urchin. And yet . . .

"I am old. Too old to look after a boy."

"And yet younger than our ancestor Sarah."

She lets loose a derisive laugh but gestures them inside. Quite suddenly, her heart feels younger. Is it the boy, the glimpse of purpose, or the mysterious presence of this man? She is lonelier than she realizes if a single visit can ease the sting of this difficult night.

She has no way of knowing the good ahead for her—that this boy will become her son, and she his mother. That in two years, he will race home with news of a resurrected king. That because of him, she will become a follower of the Way. That she will find freedom beneath a new Moses—one who passed through the waters of the Jordan in baptism, one who was tested in the wilderness but passed, one who taught the fulfillment of the Torah on the side of a mountain, one who healed and died and is even now alive.

She does not know this, and yet in the presence of this mysterious visitor, something in her spirit speaks of hope and new life in the midst of the ashes.

Reflection Questions

In what ways has God turned deep pain into an unexpected opportunity to show love or kindness to someone else?

This story is not one in the Bible, although sadly, the killing of the Bethlehem children is. Read John 20:30 and imagine another instance that could have happened but is not written of in Scripture. How can this inspire our imaginations and our faith?

Prayer

Lord God, we bring you our grief today. Our mourning for those who are no longer with us, our mourning for children not born. Give us eyes to see the beauty of your world with gratitude, even in the hard times. Father, may your Holy Spirit fill us with hope. Amen.

Suggested Reading

Matthew 2:1–18

Matthew 5:4

TWENTY-TWO

The Business of God

Inspired by Luke 10:38–42

Martha brings the ladle to her mouth and sips the lamb stew. The juices of wild onion and garlic dance with cumin and dill on her tongue. Still, it is not perfect.

She sprinkles a generous pinch of salt harvested from the Dead Sea into the stew and stirs, tasting again. "Let it simmer before dishing it," she tells one of her servants.

Beside her, another servant places a coriander relish flavored with rosemary and saffron on plates alongside flatbread warm from the oven. She grabs a waiting platter of fruit—grapes, melons, dates, figs, and cucumbers—to take to the men reclining in the next room.

The men. And one woman.

Martha bites her cheek as she glances at her sister Mary sitting at the feet of the rabbi Jesus.

She did not expect this. When she invited the teacher into her home the week before, she did not expect this at all.

She offers the platter of fruit to a man in fine clothes holding a tablet. He takes a cluster of grapes and two figs and thanks her. She smiles, forcing herself to remember her position as hostess. She will do what is required of her to honor Jesus and his followers. *She*, at least, will not disgrace their family or their guest.

Martha moves to a sturdy man who sits beside her brother Lazarus—Peter, she recalls. She thinks back to the week before, when two of Lazarus's friends had arrived in Bethany with news from Galilee—news of a highly regarded itinerant teacher, Jesus of Nazareth, who worked miracles and spoke with authority.

Martha had quickly offered their home to her brother's friends and their rabbi. She would honor Adonai in this way, as a woman should—with the domestic work of her hands, with the food she prepared, with a smile, and with gracious hospitality.

If she had known her audacious younger sister would make a mockery of their family, she might not have been so hasty to offer.

Skipping over Mary, Martha offers the platter to Jesus, who takes a melon. "Thank you, Martha." He looks into her eyes. "Your hospitality is appreciated."

She smiles, trying to hide a blush as she offers the next man food. There. The teacher said he appreciated her hospitality. Of course, he did not approve of her sister counting herself among his followers or eating among the men. Absurd! Surely, he was simply too polite to correct Mary.

When she finishes offering the platter, she glares at Mary from the corner of the room, hoping to catch her sister's gaze. But Mary has eyes only for Jesus. He is talking about praying without an audience, and although Martha is tempted to make another round with the picked-over fruit platter to hear the story, the bread is growing cool.

Besides, a woman honors Adonai with her work in the kitchen and with serving, not by sitting at the feet of a rabbi. What nerve Mary possesses to think that she, a woman, can be one of Jesus's students. Why did Lazarus not chide her? Why did the teacher not chide her? Did they not realize what a mockery Mary made of them? How would their family ever recover from such disgrace?

She counts off plates of warm bread and relish, excluding her sister. She orders a servant to flavor the cake with cinnamon and prepare it for the oven. Taking four plates at once, she directs another servant to follow her with more.

"If you forgive other people when they sin against you, your heavenly Father will also forgive you."

Something in Martha's insides pull. What has she missed? Perhaps she should have stayed and listened.

But no. This is her gift. This is how she serves Adonai. She hands a plate to the man named John.

"Lord, will you teach us how to pray?" Mary asks.

Jesus smiles at Martha's sister. "That is one thing I would be honored to do."

Martha straightens, her now-empty hands in bunched fists at her sides. Enough is enough. Mary is acting like . . . like a man. She is ignoring the work to be done. She is dishonoring these men and the teacher. She is dishonoring her family.

"Lord," Martha says. The room grows silent, every set of eyes on her, the only one standing. She does not care. "Don't you care that my sister has left me to do the work by myself? Tell her to help me!"

As soon as the words are out, she recognizes them as whiny and petulant. But someone must call out her sister's foolishness!

Jesus's eyes are kind as he looks to her. It seems he understands the turmoil in her heart.

"Martha, Martha," he says, gentle, caring. It reminds her of how Father spoke to her when she grew frustrated over her goat cheese not setting properly or her wool refusing to stay smooth during carding. "You are worried and upset about many things."

He did see into her spirit, then. For it is not only the food preparations that upset her, not only the feeding of all these men. It is the social disgrace Mary caused.

Jesus continues. "Few things are needed—indeed only one. Mary has chosen what is better, and it will not be taken away from her."

Martha blinks and nods, backing up a few steps to hide her mortification. Instead of ducking back into the kitchen, though, she slinks into a guest room and leans against the wall as Jesus continues teaching.

Part of her wants to defend herself. She is only trying to honor HaShem, after all.

But deep inside, she recognizes the truth. She is not trying to honor HaShem as much as she is trying to honor her family, as much as she is trying to honor herself.

She closes her eyes. *Adonai, forgive me.*

She replays Jesus's words over and over again. More than another plate of food, Jesus cares about his followers receiving what *he* has to offer. He is welcoming her sister alongside the men. He is validating her position at his feet, encouraging her to embrace his ways. Claiming it is better than food, even.

Martha swallows, facing the choice before her: Go back into the kitchen and improve the stew, or sit beside her sister and learn what Jesus offers that is better than food, better than the approval of neighbors, better than anything this world has to give.

Pulling in a deep breath, she walks into the sitting room and sinks onto an ornamental pillow beside Mary. Jesus looks at her so tenderly that she blinks away tears.

"This, then, is how you should pray," he says.

Martha closes her eyes and soaks up the ways of the Lord.

Reflection Questions

In Martha's time, it was unthinkable and scandalous for a woman to fulfill her duty to men and God by seeking after theology. How does Jesus break this mindset?

Luke does not tell us if Martha chooses to sit at Jesus's feet this day, but we read in John 11 that she places her faith in Jesus as the Messiah. Imagine what her journey to this realization was like.

Prayer

Lord, help us appreciate anew how scandalous your love and grace are, both in the context of the Bible and now, as you continue your work in the world and in us. Amid lives we often cultivate with busyness, give us minds and hearts for the one thing that is truly needed. Amen.

Suggested Reading

Luke 10:38–42

TWENTY-THREE

A Notorious Sinner

Inspired by Luke 19:1–10

"There he is!"

The crowd surges, swarming the road. Zacchaeus cranes his neck to glimpse the teacher, but he cannot see anything through the sea of traders, soldiers, men, and priests. If only he were a bit taller—the height of an average man, even. Perhaps then he'd be able to glimpse the rabbi from Nazareth.

"He healed the blind man outside the city gates—you know, the one who sits begging by the roadside? I saw it myself!"

"I'm bringing my honeyed pistachio pastries to the dinner tonight. I hope he likes them!"

"Do you think he will teach? I have a pain in my leg. Do you think he will heal me?"

"Could he possibly be the Messiah?"

Conversations swirl around Zacchaeus. The crowd erupts as the Galilean group rounds a feathery grove of palms.

"Jesus! Jesus!"

So many call his name. Zacchaeus forgets his dignity and jumps to see above the crowd, but he only glimpses Melech, the man who is to host the dinner that night. The tall man stands in the middle of the road, waiting for the teacher.

The crowd, now quiet and still, parts for Jesus.

Melech speaks, but Zacchaeus cannot hear the words. No doubt he invites Jesus to his home for the feast—a feast Zacchaeus will not be welcomed to join.

Though Zacchaeus cannot make out a reply, the tangible disappointment in the crowd floats back toward him. The rabbi has declined. Perhaps he already has plans closer to Yerushalayim.

Still, the crowd pushes in as the teacher continues on. Curious regret swells within Zacchaeus. He is so close, and yet he will miss his chance to glimpse the Galilean rabbi.

Desperation wells within him, along with something nameless, overwhelming, profound. He does not pause to ponder it. All he knows is he *must* see Jesus.

He turns and pushes his way out of the crowd. Someone recognizes him and spits on him. Another elbows him hard, almost knocking him to the ground. The large key to the customs booth that hangs at his neck, a mark of his standing, swings up and hits his chin. But he does not pause.

If the crowd respected him, they would part for him—a powerful, wealthy man. But they do not. He is the man who collaborates with Rome. He has burdened his people by taking more than his fair share of the taxes he's collected. He has been dishonest. Though he tries to convince himself otherwise, he deserves their gibes and ridicule.

He swallows down a date-sized lump in his throat and pushes through the outskirts of the crowd. Then he breaks into a run. His richly embroidered robe catches between his legs, but he does not pause to gird his loins. If he can get ahead of Jesus, if he can find a high spot to hide, he will be able to glimpse the could-be Messiah.

He passes the quarried ruins of the palatial retreat Herod the Great built for himself. He continues running. When he reaches a spot of empty road, he gasps for breath, his sandals dusty, the hem of his mantle dirty.

The crowd draws closer, pressing in on Jesus and his festive group. Zacchaeus searches the road, looks past an almond tree and a pair of pomegranate trees. There! A glorious sycamore about thirty cubits away, almost outside the town limits.

He runs. He has not climbed a tree since he was a boy, but when he reaches the sycamore, he scrambles up one of its wide-spreading, low branches. He hopes the dense foliage is enough to hide him. Perhaps the crowd will disperse and go feast together on the meal the teacher has declined. After Zacchaeus sees Jesus, he himself will go home to a lonely dinner.

He climbs higher, the rough bark scraping his inner thigh where his tunic bunches. He grabs his robe and positions it so anyone happening to look up will not see his indecency. His skin grows hot. What is he thinking? This is *not* how he will earn the respect of the townspeople.

But he cannot get down now—he will be spotted. Besides, he *must* see Jesus!

He peers through two branches and glimpses Jesus at the head of the group. The teacher's robes look older than Zacchaeus's finest jewels.

Some in the crowd seek the shade of the sycamore tree, and Zacchaeus stills, plastering himself to the limb. The teacher draws closer. Unexplored, foreign longing fills him. He wishes things were different. He wishes he could join the crowd. He wishes he would not be filled with shame if the Messiah saw him.

Below, an adolescent boy releases a cackle. "Look! It's the tax collector!"

Zacchaeus scrunches his eyes shut, shimmies his robe lower.

More laughter, then a man calls to him. "Did you not bring your plush pillows up there with you?"

"Where are your precious ledgers, Zacchaeus?" another calls. "Looks like the thief has finally been treed!"

There is nothing he can do but bear it, as one affront spurs on another. Jesus will witness his ridicule. He will know everything there is to know about the town tax collector.

"Zacchaeus!" a new voice calls. But it is one of authority, not ridicule.

Zacchaeus opens his eyes and sees Jesus. He braces himself for certain condemnation, his skin hot with shame. He has never been more humiliated in his life—up in this tree in his fine robes bought with the townspeople's money, facing a man he very much wants to impress.

"Zacchaeus," Jesus repeats. "Come down immediately. I must stay at your house today."

Zacchaeus blinks at the teacher, his embarrassment momentarily forgotten. "Lord?"

"I said come down. I wish to go to your house!"

He lets out a surprised gasp and wiggles down from the tree, impossible joy welling up.

Around him, the crowd mutters as he leads Jesus toward his home. "He will go and be the guest of a sinner? He will deny us but defile himself in that man's home?"

Zacchaeus senses the crowd's anger turning from him to Jesus. Gratitude washes over him.

Once they arrive at his home, his servants make quick work of preparing a lavish feast for Jesus and his followers. Some of the townsfolk come with platters and dishes in hand. Zacchaeus greets each kindly. His heart sings.

The Messiah has accepted him, has chosen him! He has made his residence one of honor and joy. He deserves none of it.

Before they sit to partake of the meal, Zacchaeus stands. "Look, Lord! Here and now, I give half of my possessions to the poor, and if I have cheated anybody out of anything, I will pay back four times the amount."

The crowd gasps. As the Lord and these people are his witness, he *will* do right. He has been shown extravagant mercy and will in turn show extravagant love to his community. He refuses to add to their burden any longer.

Jesus places his hand on Zacchaeus's shoulder. "Today salvation has come to this house because this man, too, is a son of Abraham. For the Son of Man came to seek and to save the lost."

Joy fills Zacchaeus. He was lost, unseen, unloved. But Jesus looked up into that tree and called to his heart, changing everything. He gave him an identity he longed for, one he will now step into with complete abandon.

He has been restored. He *belongs*. He is a child of the Most High.

Reflection Questions

Read Luke 18:35–43. In this story, Jesus tends to the oppressed. But in the story of Zacchaeus, Jesus is tending to the oppressor. How does this expression of love break down barriers we tend to erect?

Imagine the town after Zacchaeus carries out his promise to help the poor, pay back those he cheated, and go forth honestly in his business. How did Jesus's compassion grant healing not just to Zacchaeus but to his entire community?

Prayer

God Almighty, thank you for loving all of humanity. Give us eyes to see our neighbor. Give us courage to have hard conversations in love. Give us empathy to imagine ourselves in the shoes of others and give us grace to hear their stories. Amen.

Suggested Reading

Luke 19:1–10

TWENTY-FOUR

A Borrowed Colt

Inspired by Mark 11:1–11 and John 12:12–19

Bracha turns from packing the donkey with fresh unleavened Passover bread. She rubs one long ear of the colt, the fluffy white fur brushing her fingertips. The Muscat colt has not yet been ridden or taken the trip with her husband Gideon to the Yerushalayim marketplace. He will stay with her in Bethphage this year as Bracha sells bread at the market in preparation for the Paschal Feast.

She thinks of the whispers that the teacher, Jesus of Nazareth, is coming to Yerushalayim. That perhaps he comes as more than a common pilgrim. Her thoughts turn to the events that transpired only days before. She had seen Lazarus come out of the tomb with her own eyes. One moment they mourned, comforting Lazarus's sisters as they observed shiva—the next they fell to their knees in disbelief over the miracle the rabbi performed.

After that, both Bracha and her husband sat at the feet of the teacher. And neither will ever be the same again.

What would it be like to follow Jesus into the Holy City, to see what glorious things he might do?

But of course, she cannot go. She is needed here, in Bethphage. Many pilgrims will purchase the bread she made. They will eat it as soon as the first three stars brighten the night sky tomorrow evening. And she and Gideon need the income to survive the rest of the year.

She startles at a poke in her side and turns to see her husband grinning down at her. “Gideon!”

He nuzzles his face to her neck. “My wife is daydreaming once again.”

She smiles but pulls away from him. It would not be proper for the neighbors to see. “How can I not? The town is afire with anticipation. Do you think he will come?”

“I can think of little else but sitting beneath his teaching again,” her husband confesses.

Her heart spills over. “Me, too.”

He pulls her into their home. “Come inside so I may kiss you goodbye without the neighbors watching.”

She willingly goes with him, sinking into his arms. He runs a hand over the slight bulge of her stomach. “Next time this year, Bracha, we will have a child to teach the Passover traditions. Perhaps they will someday sit at the temple, beneath the teaching of Jesus.”

Bracha cannot imagine anything better.

Their donkey brays. “I best make my way,” Gideon says.

“Me, too. I meant to be at the market by now.”

They step out of their home. Bracha gasps at the sight of two familiar men untying their colt.

Gideon steps forward. “John? Peter? What are you doing, untying our colt?”

John's pleasant face reddens. "We did not wish to bother you." Bracha's own skin heats that Jesus's two disciples had obviously seen her and Gideon's private moment in their home. "The Lord has need of the colt and will send it back shortly."

The back of Bracha's neck prickles. Jesus had need of their colt? "Of course," she says. "Does he have need of our donkey as well?" Then, realizing what she has offered, gives her husband a sheepish look. Without the donkey, it will be impossible for Gideon to take their bread to Yerushalayim.

But her husband nods. "Yes, if the Lord has need of it, he must have it."

Peter shakes his head. "The colt is all that is needed. Thank you."

The disciples lead their colt away. Bracha meets her husband's gaze, her heart pulling to follow—not to tend to their colt but to see Jesus again.

He squeezes her hand. "Perhaps you could accompany me to Yerushalayim today?"

She throws her arms around his neck, no longer caring what neighbors see. They will take a steep loss not selling in their own marketplace, but as far as she is concerned, Jesus is worth it.

A short time later, they drop off their bread with another pastry maker who agrees to sell it in the Bethphage market and split the profits. Then they chase after Peter and John.

Soon, they are caught in a crowd coming from the city. Many hold palm branches, making their way not to the temple but to Jesus. In the distance, another throng walks down the winding caravan road. Lambs destined for the temple altar surround them, some walking, some in the arms of travelers. There will be more once they near the city, hundreds of spotless, bleating lambs driven into Yerushalayim by way of the Sheep Gate. The crowd swells with anticipation, the multitude waving palm branches.

"It is him!"

"It is Jesus of Nazareth!"

"He must be the Messiah!"

Bracha's stomach quivers. The Judaean land is vivid today, dips of red silt mixed with a tawny hue that reminds her of a lion's coat. Peter and John lay their cloaks upon the colt. A solemn-looking Jesus mounts the animal. Bracha squeezes Gideon's arm, anticipating that the colt, never ridden, will be frantic. But it accepts the burden as easily as Gideon had offered their donkey.

Tears prick Bracha's eyes. She is overwhelmed by seeing this mighty man of HaShem on their humble animal.

"Do not be afraid, daughter of Zion," Gideon whispers. "See, your king is coming, seated on a donkey's colt."

Those around Gideon catch wind of his words and more bold proclamations that Jesus is the Messiah come to save them from Rome surge above the noise. It is as if fire leaps from spirit to spirit, the anticipation of the Messiah's kingdom so close each can taste it.

The two crowds merge together and turn as one toward the Holy City, moving unhurriedly down the Mount of Olives. The southeastern corner of the city gleams above them, glowing like a bride readied for her king. The temple stretches golden tips into the heavens. Only a Sabbath day's journey away from the city now, the crowd rejoices, praising Adonai as they throw their cloaks in front of the colt to create a royal carpet. Others spread palms and branches they cut from the fields before Jesus.

"Hosanna!" they cry above the bleating of the lambs.

Save us.

The green tips of palm branches, the symbol of Judea, fringe the cobalt sky. The sight calls to mind the revolt led by Judas Maccabee less than two centuries before—a revolt that liberated the temple.

"Blessed is he who comes in the name of the Lord!"

"Blessed is the womb that bore you!"

"Hosanna in the highest heaven!"

Bracha is caught up in it—part patriotic fervor and longing for her people to be free from beneath the Romans, and part anticipation over what Jesus, a man who raises the dead and speaks powerfully of HaShem, will do to make that happen.

The crowd sings out the Psalms of Ascent. They end on the reminder of God's enduring love.

Gideon takes her hand as they follow. His tone sobers. "Pilate will be in the city."

To supervise over the Feast, no doubt. She thinks on the procurator's past deeds—the placement of shields bearing the portrait of the emperor in the temple by night, the stealing from the temple treasury in order to build an aqueduct, and then disguising his soldiers as Jews to attack the disgruntled crowd when they protested. Will there be conflict now? Does Gideon regret allowing her to come?

She places a protective hand over her swollen belly as they pass beneath the Golden Gate. The crowd squeezes, packed like sardines in a lunch basket. The donkey Gideon leads bobs its head, irritated by the mass of people. Alongside sheep and cattle, lambs are everywhere. Bracha clings to her husband's fingers.

A stranger grabs Gideon's arm. "Who is this?" He gestures ahead to their rabbi.

"Have you not heard? This is Jesus, the prophet from Nazareth in Galilee. The one who raises the dead!" Gideon answers.

Beside him, two men in the long robes of Pharisees elbow each other. "See how the whole world has gone after him!"

Bracha swallows. A foreboding darkens the air of festivity. Jesus *is* the Messiah, but she fears for him. He has no formed army. He is riding not on a war horse but on a lowly colt. Pilate is here to remind the people that Rome is in charge.

Yet, surely a man who raises the dead will be able to deliver the city from Caesar's yoke?

She watches a stray lamb escape from its master and flee the crowd. She watches Jesus's meek form enter Yerushalayim on their colt. She remembers how Herod killed Jesus's cousin, John the Baptizer.

They all expect the Messiah to come in the same manner as Judas Maccabee, but Jesus is defying their expectations at every turn. What can it all mean?

Reflection Questions

The crowd expects Jesus to overthrow Rome, but he comes riding on an animal that one would not expect for a warrior. Aside from fulfilling the prophecy in Zechariah 9:9, what do you think Jesus intended with the use of the colt? What was he modeling for us?

Imagine yourself a follower of Jesus in this crowd, longing for freedom. What does this tell you about the human heart? About your own heart?

Prayer

Heavenly Father, thank you for coming into the world, for writing such an unlikely story that we only have to look to history to see your thumbprint and the orchestration of your majesty. You were meek in your birth and meek when ushering in your kingdom. May we remember your gentle lowliness as we work out what it is to be fully human. Blessed are you, Lord, and blessed are we to be so loved by you. Amen.

Suggested Reading

Psalm 118
Mark 11:1–11
Matthew 21:1–11
Luke 19: 28–44
John 12:12–19

TWENTY-FIVE

Of Utmost Importance

Inspired by Mark 12:18–34

He is not supposed to have questions, of course. He is to answer the questions.

As a doctor of the law, a scribe, Amos answers questions all day. When he asks a question, it is usually to goad the Sadducees in a debate. Little boys ask questions to learn. Grown men and teachers ask questions to illuminate a wrong way of belief—to discredit another's teaching.

Amos enters the temple and looks to the many men, women, and children in the Court of the Gentiles. His gaze lands on a crowd of men in garb similar to his own—Pharisees and Sadducees—beneath the eastern colonnade of Solomon's Porch.

From the law to politics to the Romans who occupy their land, the differing views among the two groups make Amos's head swirl. He has worked closely with them in the Sanhedrin. Perhaps someday he will earn a seat alongside these men—men who serve not only as esteemed teachers but as a court of law and political council.

He scolds himself for the ambitious thought. His desire to understand HaShem and draw closer to him encouraged Amos to study the law with fervor as a boy. To inspect and evaluate its smallest parts, to draw from it the secret messages of life. To pore over and uphold its 613 doctrines and to decipher the quieter parts. When had his yearning morphed into personal aspiration?

He *must* remember his first love.

Amos glimpses a man in plain dress at the center of the group—the Galilean from Nazareth? Jesus? Amos heard about the rabbi overturning the tables of the money changers the day before. He had rebuked the teachers for imprudent fripperies such as the tithing of cumin and dill.

Amos draws closer. A member of the Sadducees named Osher speaks to Jesus. "Teacher, Moses wrote for us that if a man's brother dies and leaves a wife but no children, the man must marry the widow and raise up offspring for his brother." The other members of the Sadducees stand behind him, nodding. "Now, say there were seven brothers. The first one married and died without leaving any children. The second one married the widow, but he also died, leaving no child. It was the same with the third. In fact, none of the seven left any children. Last of all, the woman died too. At the resurrection, whose wife will she be, since the seven were married to her?"

Amos holds back a snort at the ridiculous question. Leave it to Osher to come up with such a riddle to try and discredit the resurrection.

Jesus cocks his head, studying Osher and the others who fold their arms in challenge. "Are you not in error because you do not know the Scriptures or the power of God?"

A tune of victory plays across Amos's heart. Jesus is on the side of the Pharisees and the resurrection, then.

He continues. "When the dead rise, they will neither marry nor be given in marriage; they will be like the angels in heaven. Now about the dead rising—have you not read in the Book of Moses, in the account of the burning bush, how God said to him, 'I am the God of Abraham, Isaac, and Jacob'? He is not the God of the dead, but of the living. You are badly mistaken!"

The rabbi speaks with authority. Jesus has purposefully appealed to the Torah instead of to the Prophets, as the Sadducees do not give the Prophets their due. He is saying that the coming world is not a replica of this world—it is more. God will work in more stupendous ways than any of them imagine. He will not leave their ancestors Abraham, Isaac, and Jacob dead, and perhaps he will not leave them dead either.

The Sadducees talk among themselves. Amos can practically see their tunics in a bunch. The Pharisees, for their part, seem speechless, even though Jesus has, in a sense, sided with them.

Hungry to hear more, Amos thrusts himself through the crowd. He will ask Jesus a question he has struggled with—ask it as a boy asks his rabbi or his father, not as a well-respected scribe challenges a peer.

"Teacher, of all the commandments, which is the most important?"

He longs to know. Does Jesus have an answer?

The teacher does not hesitate. "The most important one is this: 'Hear, O Israel: The Lord our God, the Lord is one. Love the Lord your God with all your heart and with all your soul and with all your mind and with all your strength.' The second is this: 'Love your neighbor as yourself.' There is no commandment greater than these."

Amos's heart sings. Another unexpected answer that finds purchase in the depths of his soul, in the deep roots of his people. For did not these two commandments summarize the entirety of the law? Jesus had returned them to the Shema, the oft-recited words never far from any Hebrew's lips, whether strong and living or weak and readying for death. But Jesus has gone further to encompass the nature of God himself—love. Love to God, love to humanity.

"Well said, teacher." Amos speaks with warm authenticity. He no longer cares if the members of the Sanhedrin think he should test this man. From Jesus's answers, Amos knows that even he, well-versed in the law, will never win a debate against him. And what does any of it matter if true teaching goes forth? "You are right in saying that God is one and there is no other but him. To love him with all your heart, with all your understanding and with all your strength, and to love your neighbor as yourself is more important than all burnt offerings and sacrifices."

A small smile curves Jesus's lips. "You are not far from the kingdom of God."

Neither group moves to ask more questions. Instead, they disperse. Amos lingers with Jesus and his disciples, pondering the moral beauty of the law anew.

He is not far from the kingdom of God. He has an inkling that to be even closer, he must draw nearer to this teacher.

Reflection Questions

What might have hindered a Pharisee from coming to Jesus? In the same way, what might hinder the "religious" among us today in seeing God?

Jesus taught that all the commandments hold a living connection with these two "great" commandments—loving God and loving others. How does this make sense to you? In what way do you struggle to grasp his words?

Prayer

God Almighty, thank you for coming to earth to demonstrate and fulfill the law so perfectly and completely. Help us not only to embrace the mystery of our faith but to also embrace our God-given curiosity of being human, of wanting answers. May we find peace in between. Amen.

Suggested Reading

Mark 12:18–34

Matthew 22:23–40

TWENTY-SIX

All She Has

Inspired by Mark 12:38–44

Ten years is too long.

Tirzah climbs the steps of the Beautiful Gate, taking in the glistening limestone and lavish marble of the temple. Her heart warms as she enters the grand folds of Adonai's dwelling place. The last time she journeyed to the Holy City for the Paschal Feast, Phineas had been alive and well.

How would her life be different if she had borne a child? How would her life be different if Phineas had been well the last nine years of his existence?

She sighs. There is no use dwelling on what might have been. Adonai has sustained her, both in the spiritual and the physical. Tirzah finds comfort in prayer and a meager livelihood with the making of her baskets. She even sold a basket earlier today to a man peddling similar goods in the Yerushalayim marketplace. The businessman looked over the intricate weaving of the reeds—reeds she had picked and soaked and woven with painstaking care. He offered her a less than fair price, but since she had spent the last of her coins to travel from Bethsaida, she accepted the number. She had no choice if she wished to offer her Passover sacrifice.

After she gives the sum of the two doves, she will be left with only a half shekel, destined for the temple tax, and two prutahs. The two coins are not nearly enough for her journey home but now they are all she has.

Pocketing the coins, she savors each step into the temple. Inside the Court of Women, incense mixes with the perfumes of travelers. Worshipers linger for devotion and sacrifices. Walking through the Nicanor Gate and into the Court of the Israelites, she sees an ornate opened door, the entrance to the Holy Place.

Tirzah's gaze lingers on the thick curtain beyond the door before she turns her attention to the thirteen trumpet-shaped boxes beneath the colonnade. She watches as men in flowing robes walk from one box to the next, glancing at the inscriptions on each before casting their riches into the chests.

Her stomach twists. If only she could give more. If only she appeared more presentable, in a garment other than this sackcloth of mourning.

Ten years is too long, and two coins are not enough. But Adonai, who knows the heart, will surely see she longs to give more, that she would linger in his house all the days of her life if she could. No matter that she cannot get closer to the Most Holy Place than the Court of Women allows—she is closer to him now than in Bethsaida.

Tirzah crosses the court and seeks the boxes beside the Shushan Gate, choosing one into which to deposit her half shekel for her annual temple tribute. She inserts the coin into the narrow mouth of the trumpet and listens to it fall onto others inside the wide base. Filled with gratitude, she moves on to the next box and deposits the sum for two turtledoves. The entirety of the box will be taken out by the priests at the end of the day and the corresponding number of doves offered.

The remaining two prutahs clink together in her purse—the last of her earthly wealth.

She passes the other boxes, ignoring the smug look of one man in a long embroidered robe carrying a heavy purse and strolling with a self-important swagger. He sneers at her as he places a hefty handful of coins into the fifth trumpet-shaped box, designated for wood used for the temple sacrifices.

The man moves on to the next chest, this one designated for temple incense. The silver lands with a satisfying tinkle in the bottom, signaling that a large donation was given. This man has made a difference in HaShem's kingdom.

He moves on to the next box, and the next. Tirzah forces her gaze from him and walks to one of the last boxes, set aside for general offerings. She digs out her last two coins from her purse and blinks back tears. She could give only one, but something compels her to reach out and deposit them both in the mouth of the trumpet. She barely hears them fall inside the box.

It is not much, but now she has given Adonai all she has.

Warmth tunnels through her. A long-forgotten joy roots in the depth of her being.

She senses someone watching and turns to glimpse a man in a simple flax robe teaching on the steps. He looks at her, but not as the man with the luxurious robes looked at her in front of the treasury boxes. He looks at her as if he sees *within* her—past her humble mourning dress and maybe even past her meager offering. He nods at her, and the small gesture fills her heart. She cannot explain it, but it feels like an affirmation, as if he understands the cost of what she has done.

Tirzah gives him a smile before climbing the stairs to the raised dais that the women worship upon. Perhaps she will seek out the man and hear his teachings a bit later.

For now, she will worship HaShem, the one who has shown her the beauty of humble love. She will lean not into the assurance of a big donation or lavish displays of giving—she will lean into his arms alone.

Reflection Questions

Read Matthew 6:1–6. How does the silent and humble worship of this woman align with what Jesus teaches in this section of the Sermon on the Mount?

Very soon, Jesus will empty himself and give his whole life for his children. How is the widow in this story like Jesus in what she gives?

Prayer

All-seeing Savior, you know all. From every action and inaction to every good deed or careless remark uttered. You see the depths of our hearts—both the good and the bruised. Thank you for loving us into communion with you. May we look to your example and your words to inspire us to deeper faith in you. Amen.

Suggested Reading

Mark 12:38–44

Luke 20:45–21:4

TWENTY-SEVEN

Asleep in the Garden

Inspired by Matthew 26:36–46 and Mark 14:32–42

The words of the psalm swirl in James's mind as he accompanies Jesus and the other disciples through the streets of Yerushalayim.

When hard pressed, I cried to the LORD;
he brought me into a spacious place.
The LORD is with me: I will not be afraid.

The cobblestone streets, cut into steps, are far from empty. Merry lamplight brightens the borders of shuttered windows and closed doors as city dwellers entertain guests for the Passover celebration. Some prepare for temple, the gates of which will open on the midnight watch. The foul odor of burning flesh from the sacrificial lambs saturates the city.

The somber group exits the gate north of the temple and descends into the black valley of the Kidron. James's gaze rests on Jesus. The festive glow of the city grows dimmer with each step. Light from James's lamp bounces off rocks and dirt. In the distance, hundreds of pilgrim campfires dot the valley. The scent of roasted lamb permeates the air even here.

They cross the Brook Kidron. Tonight, it is red from the blood of the thousands of lambs offered that day.

James shivers. He thinks of the events of the last several days—of Lazarus walking out of his family tomb in graveclothes, of his sister Mary pouring an entire jar of spikenard onto their rabbi's head, of Jesus riding into the city on the colt amid wails of praise and waving of palms, of Jesus just hours ago lifting a copper cup of wine and proclaiming it his blood poured out for them.

Emotion builds in James's throat as he remembers Jesus's head bent over a bowl of water at James's feet, his hands upon his soles. Jesus called him and John Sons of Thunder. Their father, Zebedee, had quite liked that.

Now, though, James is uncertain he should have claimed the title with such pride.

Unbidden, other words of Jesus's come to mind. Words far less pleasant than a half-joking nickname.

The Son of Man is going to be delivered into the hands of men. They will kill him, and after three days he will rise.

What did Jesus mean?

James hadn't asked his rabbi to explain, and neither had the others. Jesus came to Yerushalayim to usher in his kingdom, after all. Why then, did his most recent words ring of weighty goodbyes and solemn farewells?

Jesus's tired form slumps as they approach the base of the Mount of Olives—certainly not the countenance of a man about to claim a kingship.

Unspoken and unanswered questions consume James.

At the gate of Gethsemane, Jesus gestures to James, Peter, and John. "Come." To the others, he says, "Sit here while I go over there and pray." He points to a place in the corner of the garden, past the fruit trees and flowering shrubs, to a patch of earth where they have gathered on previous visits to the Holy City.

James follows his brother, Peter, and Jesus into the garden. Scant moonlight shines on the stones of the ancient olive press for which the peaceful garden is named.

It is just the four of them. As it was when Jesus took the hand of Jairus's daughter and called her out of her deathly sleep. As it was when they climbed Mount Tabor and their rabbi's face shone like the sun, his clothes a blinding white.

James must remember those moments when the tempter threatens to enfold him. But if Jesus leaves them, how can they move forward? They have abandoned everything for him. What would a future without their beloved rabbi look like?

As they walk, Jesus's sorrow turns palpable, crushing James like that old olive press used to crush the delicate skins of olives. Jesus stops at a fig tree. "My soul is overwhelmed with sorrow to the point of death. Stay here and keep watch."

With burdened steps, Jesus stumbles a little farther before collapsing on the ground, arms splayed in supplication. "Abba," he prays. "Everything is possible for you."

James sits alongside Peter and John, their backs resting against a gnarled olive tree.

"We will also pray," Peter says, but only a short time later James hears the heavy breathing of sleep from both his brother and Peter.

He glances at Jesus, who has sweat like blood upon his brow. He hears his whispered pleas winding through the fruit trees, weaving with the sweet, tangy scent of pomegranate blossoms. Immense grief overtakes James. All he wants to do is sleep away the sadness. Perhaps he will wake and find this all a dream. Perhaps he will wake on Mount Tabor again, in the presence of HaShem.

His eyelids grow heavy.

He jolts awake at the sound of Jesus's voice. "Couldn't you men keep watch with me for one hour? Watch and pray so that you will not fall into temptation. The spirit is willing, but the flesh is weak."

James sits up. Pray for themselves? What is in store for them?

Jesus again goes to pray. He looks to the star-studded sky, his face twisted in agony. "Abba, if it is not possible for this cup to be taken away unless I drink it, may your will be done."

This is my blood of the covenant, which is poured out for many for the forgiveness of sins.

James prays with Peter and John for a long while. They pray for their master's spirit to be renewed with the strength the prophet Isaiah spoke of. They pray for themselves, as Jesus instructed.

But the night wears on, their prayers becoming few and far between, emotion and exhaustion clinging to them like a wet goat hair blanket.

James's eyes again droop, but he sits up, remembering how Jesus rebuked him and John when they asked to be seated at his right and left hand, how he chastised them when they wanted to rain down fire on the Samaritan village that had not welcomed their teacher.

He will not let Jesus down again. Not this time.

He prays for a long time, but the warmth of John's body lures him to slump against his brother. He closes his eyes for only a moment . . .

"Are you still sleeping and resting?"

James sits upright, wipes a stream of drool from the side of his mouth. "Forgive us, master."

But Jesus does not seem upset. In fact, the sorrow that clung to him is no longer present. Like Jacob, it seems he has wrestled a blessing from Adonai.

Would all be okay, then?

Jesus points toward the gate. "Look, the hour has come and the Son of Man is delivered into the hands of sinners. Rise, let us go. Here comes my betrayer."

James pushes away the dregs of sleep, fully awake at the heavy march of men carrying lanterns and torches, swords and clubs. And at the front, one of their very own.

Judas ben Iscariot.

That pigeon-hearted son of a camel.

Peter reaches for his sword, and James does the same. Where is Simon the Zealot when they need him?

Jesus had asked them to keep watch, to stay awake, to pray for strength. And they have once again failed.

What price will they pay for their sorrowful sleep?

Reflection Questions

Contrast the opportunity of everlasting life that Adam of Genesis was given in the garden of Eden with the opportunity Jesus is given in the garden of Gethsemane. How does

Jesus, in his humanity, submit to his own divinity? What does this accomplish that Adam in Eden did not?

Read Acts 12:1–5, imagining what James's faith at the end of his life was like. What do you think changed for him? What place did God's grace and the Holy Spirit play in that change?

Prayer

Abba Father, thank you for your patience with us. Thank you for the presence of your Holy Spirit to guide us. Give us wisdom to know when to rest and when to keep watch, when to slumber and when to stay alert. Thank you for who you are—a God of great forgiveness. Amen.

Suggested Reading

Matthew 26:36–46

Mark 14:12–42

Acts 12:1–5

TWENTY-EIGHT

Slave of the Most High

Inspired by Luke 22:47-53 and John 18:1-11

It would be good if one man died for the people.

Malchus grips the torch he carries, making way for the man named Judas ben Iscariot to lead their contingent up the outside stairs of the home where Jesus of Nazareth is said to reside for the Passover Seder.

The words of his master, High Priest Caiaphas, echo in his head, propelling him toward his duty.

It would be good if one man died for the people.

Caiaphas had laid a hand on Malchus's shoulder when he said that, the force of the words belying the gentle touch.

Malchus's master did not often pay him mind. But hours earlier, he had bestowed an important mission upon him, the words and the touch communicating the weight of the order.

Not to mention the company—officials from the Sanhedrin along with a detachment of Roman soldiers fresh from the fortress of Antonia, clad in leather armor, daggers at their belts. Surely, the man they seek *must* be apprehended.

For the good of the people.

Judas stumbles out of the room, his face pasty beneath the light of Malchus's torch. "They are no longer here."

Malchus squints at Judas. The man's eye twitches. There is something unhinged about this student who turns his rabbi in to the authorities. "Where could they have gone?"

Judas looks past the city gates to the Kidron Valley. "I think I know."

"Make haste, then." Malchus turns to the soldier behind him. "Follow him."

Judas leads them through the Upper City and past the temple. The boots of the soldiers clank on the constricted cobble streets. The smell of cooking grease mingles with the acrid scent of burnt flesh and incense from the temple sacrifices. The lights of the fortress glow in the distance as they enter the Kidron.

They move as one, their lanterns and torches many. They will not return unless it is with Jesus of Nazareth. No doubt the man is hiding—they will search every corner and hollow until they find him.

A cloud passes over the moon as they approach a garden on the Mount of Olives. Judas walks by a group of Galileans resting outside the garden gate. One rouses, calling to him. "Judas . . . what is the meaning of this?"

But Judas continues walking. Malchus follows, marching past an old olive press. The sheath of his sword slaps his leg. Sudden energy courses through his body. His duties normally include following Caiaphas, seeing to his safety and needs.

This mission is altogether different. Perhaps his master will see his value and bestow a gift upon him after his success.

"Once we find him, step aside for us to seize him," Malchus orders.

"I know, I know." Judas appears as ornery as a housewife who went to market without a coin purse.

The soldier behind them instructs others to search the caverns and bushes of the garden. There are many places one can hide.

"He is there," Judas says.

Malchus sees four men ahead, one in front of the others standing straight and ready. Surely this composed man is not the one named Jesus?

"Rabbi!" Judas's forced tone comes out unusually spry. He greets the man in front with a kiss on the hand, as if it weren't unusual to happen upon him in this dark garden with a fleet of guards and soldiers.

Jesus of Nazareth stares at Judas, but it is not with the fire one might expect from a dangerous rebel. "Judas, are you betraying the Son of Man with a kiss?" He turns to the soldiers and temple officials beside Malchus. "Who is it you want?"

"Jesus of Nazareth!" shouts a particularly eager Roman.

The man steps forward. "I am he."

It is as if a gust of wind pushes Malchus back with the words, forcing him to his knees.

I am he.

He expected a runaway ruffian. Who is this confident figure who meets them and speaks in the language of HaShem? Even now, Malchus struggles to stand, uneasy misgiving swirling in his chest.

Are they right to arrest Jesus?

But of course they must. Malchus is the servant of the high priest, after all, doing the bidding of his master. HaShem himself has appointed Caiaphas to mediate between Adonai and men. The high priest is set apart, the head of the priestly caste and anointed with the same holy oil as King Solomon. Caiaphas is the only one to enter the Most Holy Place. Even if his appointment had been the result of political elbow-rubbing and bribery, he holds the most esteemed position of the Israelites. Malchus need not distrust him.

"Who is it you want?" Jesus asks again.

The same Roman pulls himself to his feet alongside Malchus. He shouts all the louder. "Jesus of Nazareth!"

"I told you that I am he. If you are looking for me, then let these men go." The Nazarene's face is calm as he speaks words that protect his disciples.

Malchus glances at the three men beside Jesus—a burly man with an unsheathed sword glinting beneath torchlight, and two men with similar ruddy complexions.

This is not what Malchus anticipated.

The soldiers stride toward Jesus, and Malchus follows. He must carry out his orders.

A flash of metal beneath moonlight slices the air. Stinging pain burns a line along the right side of Malchus's head. His hand flies to the spot and comes away bloody. His ear rings, or . . . beneath the glow of lanterns, he glimpses an ear on the ground.

His ear.

He gasps, falling to his knees.

"No more of this!" Jesus kneels, facing Malchus. He places his hand on the gushing spot on the side of his head. He closes his eyes as if in prayer.

When the man's hand comes away, the pain is gone. Malchus touches his head, expecting blood, but his fingers graze the lobe of his ear. He hears. It is as if the disciple never used his weapon at all.

How is this possible?

Jesus turns to his follower. "Put your sword away! Shall I not drink the cup my Father has given me?"

His Father . . .

The soldiers bind Jesus, who willingly gives himself over as his followers flee. The cowards. Malchus stands but cannot take part in the arrest.

The soldiers lead Jesus away. Malchus feels his ear again, looks at the sword now lying on the ground, shimmering with his blood.

Who is this Jesus of Nazareth, who commands his followers not to fight for him? This man who heals his enemies in miraculous ways?

More importantly, how can Malchus heed Caiaphas's orders now that he has encountered this rabbi for himself?

Reflection Questions

This is the last of Jesus's miracles recorded before his death. Malchus may have been the last person to feel Jesus's touch before his crucifixion. Meditate on how this may have affected Malchus, both on this day and in the future.

Think of those who have been hurt by Christians over the course of history and in your lifetime. How would Jesus have us repair these relationships?

Prayer

Healing HaShem, help us be agents of healing in your world. Amid strife, political tensions, and real hurt, may we glimpse the grander vision you have for your followers. May we possess your mind and heart when dealing with our enemies. May we grow into people who mirror your grace, your kindness, your love. Amen.

Suggested Reading

Luke 22:47–53
John 18:1–11

TWENTY-NINE

Naked Shame

Inspired by Mark 10:17–22 and Mark 14:43–52

Dressed in his fine linen garment, Baruch pushes through the crowded city. Pilgrims with overflowing bags and lambs and ox carts seek shelter for the night. He was told the man named Jesus was somewhere in the Upper City taking part in the Passover Feast. He must find him.

He walks with a light step, his elaborately adorned outer garment and precious jewels no longer weighing him down. He thinks back to his encounter with Jesus two weeks ago.

"Good teacher, what must I do to inherit eternal life?"

"Why do you call me good? No one is good—except God alone. You know the commandments: 'You shall not murder, you shall not commit adultery, you shall not steal, you shall not give false testimony, you shall not defraud, honor your father and mother.'"

All the commands that emphasize relationship with others.

Baruch answered confidently. "Teacher, all these I have kept since I was a boy."

He had no regrets in all his seventeen years.

Jesus looked at him with such compassion, it made Baruch uncomfortable.

"One thing you lack," Jesus said. "Go, sell everything you have and give to the poor, and you will have treasure in heaven. Then come, follow me."

The words sucked every bit of hope from Baruch. His face fell. He thought of his parents' recent deaths, of the many vineyards and groves they had left in his care. It all turned a heavy profit each year. He would never have to worry a day in his life.

That is the thought he fell asleep to every night. That is the thought that gave him security, safety.

As much as one could hold in this life, anyway.

He turned away from the teacher that day, crushed by unbearable sadness.

When he returned to his plentiful ledgers and managers and servants, he attempted to shake off the sadness with fine wine and good friends. He went to the market and ordered a new, ornate desk.

But the sadness remained.

Baruch had stared into his empty wine cup one afternoon when a friend brought news of the rabbi named Jesus raising a man of Bethany from the dead. He exchanged sleep for prayer that night. Jesus's words echoed in his spirit.

Go, sell everything you have and give to the poor, and you will have treasure in heaven. Then come, follow me.

Even when he tried to push them aside, the words poked through, like a stubborn crocus in late Shevat.

Somewhere around the eleventh hour, Baruch stopped wrestling and surrendered.

He woke with renewed purpose.

The following morning, he called his most trusted steward to him. He paid the man a handsome sum and instructed him to sell off his property and possessions, giving the proceeds to the poor.

This very morning, Baruch left his childhood home with only his inner garment, a fine linen tunic his mother gifted him on his last birthday.

It is his only possession.

That, and the treasure in heaven Jesus spoke of. The treasure he now possesses.

As night falls upon the city, Baruch finds the home of which Martha of Bethany spoke. He raises his hand to knock, but before he can, a group of familiar Galilean men come down the stairs with lanterns. Two have swords.

He swallows down his doubts. Will the teacher remember him? Will he recognize him without his long robes and jewels?

He straightens when Jesus descends the stairs. The rabbi's face is downcast, but still he stops.

When Baruch falls at his feet this time, it is not to gain favor but to surrender.

"Teacher, I have sold everything and have come to follow you."

Jesus's smile brightens his solemn countenance.

"Am I too late, master?"

"No, my son. You are just in time. Come."

There is a different aura to the group than the first time—a heaviness, an uncertainty. They tramp through the city and Kidron Valley to a garden. Baruch waits at the gate with most of the disciples.

Perhaps this is how they spend their nights—keeping watch while Jesus prays. It will take some getting used to, but it is a small inconvenience if it means following the teacher.

When the guards and soldiers come with swords and torches, the others seem as perplexed as Baruch is.

They follow the guards to Jesus. Words are exchanged. The one named Peter takes out a sword. A tussle ensues. The disciples flee.

Terror climbs Baruch's throat. He does not understand. He has left everything. How can this be the treasure of heaven?

One of the soldiers reaches out to grab him but Baruch twists away. He bends and writhes beneath the hard hands, wriggling out of his tunic and fleeing into a copse of fruit trees.

The branches poke his bare skin. He burrows near the base of the tree, curled around himself, waiting for the lanterns and torches to disappear.

They do. And so does Jesus.

Shame rolls over him, not only because he is naked but because he is a coward to have so quickly abandoned the teacher. Was it all a mistake?

No, seeing the poor of his town well fed and clothed filled an emptiness inside him with purpose and hope, a more exciting mission and life.

But what of the fate of Jesus?

Before the sun rises from behind the blackened mountains of Moab, Baruch ventures far from the garden—exposed, humiliated.

When he comes upon a line of clothes drying in the morning sun, he snatches a coarse goatskin blanket and wraps it around himself. He stands at the city gates, begging for coins from the many pilgrims. One man gives him an extra tunic.

He follows a crowd to Golgotha. He sees his teacher hanging on a cross, forgiving sins, giving up his last breath. Darkness overcomes the land. Women weep. Baruch weeps.

A Roman soldier with gold trimmings on his breastplate looks up at Jesus's bruised and bloodied frame. "Surely this man was the Son of God!"

And Baruch knows the soldier is right.

He goes to John and Jesus's mother and Mary and Aliza and Salome and the many other women. He does not know where to flee, but he knows these people also love Jesus. They also claimed him as their treasure.

It is the only place Baruch wants to be.

Reflection Questions

There is no evidence that this man in the Gospel of Mark is the rich young ruler who comes to Jesus in Mark 10. Nevertheless, his identity does not matter. What he is remembered for is fleeing instead of following. Put yourself in this man's sandals that night (and the sandals of the other disciples). Why do you think they fled? What would it have taken for them to stand by Jesus's side during his darkest hour?

Like Adam and Eve, this man finds himself naked in a garden and filled with shame. How does God fully see him—when he first comes to Jesus, when he follows him, and when he flees?

Prayer

All-seeing Father, you are fully divine even as you stepped into humanity. As we strive to grasp what that beautiful reality means for us, help us cling to that which we know and hold with an open hand that which we don't. Sustain us, Lord. Amen.

Suggested Reading

Mark 10:17–22

Mark 14:43–52

THIRTY

Pick Up Your Cross

Inspired by Mark 15:21–32

He holds the memory of that hour with an odd mixture of shame and gratitude, never fully sinking into it and yet never separating himself from it either.

And now his boys are asking about that hour. An hour that has come to define him.

Though uncomfortable to relive, the story is one he must pass on to his children. In many ways, it is his legacy.

"Abba, please tell us." Simon's youngest, Rufus, looks over the single candle on their table. The round face of a boy is narrowing into that of an older youth.

"Yes, Abba. We are no longer children. We wish to know." Alexander speaks with the authority of an adolescent on the brink of manhood. Simon looks to Rachel, who nods encouragement.

His gaze travels to their packed bags. Tomorrow they will travel to Yerushalayim for the Passover Feast and stay until Shavuot. The season brings memories of a year ago tunneling back. The beam heavy upon his shoulders. The weakened form of the man in front of him. Peter's bold words on Shavuot that prompted a holy burning in his spirit.

But God raised him from the dead, freeing him from the agony of death, because it was impossible for death to keep its hold on him.

Simon had willingly accepted the waters of baptism the day he heard Peter, as had his wife and sons.

How much easier to remember that memory, and not the horror of the memory that preceded it? Yet without the horror, there is no miracle. There is no Holy Spirit. There is no dwelling of Adonai in hearts.

Simon swallows and nods. The boys wiggle in their seats like children of six instead of twelve and fourteen, but he does not chastise them.

"You remember how we were late coming into the Holy City for the Paschal Feast because of your grandfather's shiva."

The boys grow solemn. Simon still fights emotion when thinking of his father's unexpected demise. His heart had not been prepared to celebrate Passover last year, yet he packed his family and his widowed mother to make the long trip from Cyrene to Yerushalayim. More than ever, they needed the reminder of HaShem's deliverance. They needed to see the Holy City shining in the light of morning that Passover day. So, they joined the many pilgrims journeying to Yerushalayim—pilgrims from as far as Greece and Rome, Babylon and Alexandria.

But just outside the gates of the city, a contingent of Roman soldiers met them. The soldiers' hobnailed boots clacked against cobbles as they led three prisoners to their execution stakes. One wizened legionnaire called to Simon.

Simon clears his throat, deciding he will be transparent with his boys. "When that soldier seized me, I almost tried to refuse," he admits. "I was tired from grief and from our journey. I wanted rest."

"They made you carry the crossbeam." Alexander's face grows hard. "I wanted to help you, but you made me stay with Ima."

"Yes. I did not want you to see the horrors of crucifixion." Simon remembers looking at the bruised and bloodied face of the first prisoner. He'd ordered his wife to continue into the city with their boys and his mother.

"I wondered what this man had done to deserve such a beating. Blood soaked his garments, and I did not see how he had carried his cross ten cubits. But even then, I did not feel sorry for him. In fact, I resented his crimes and the soldiers, who delayed me celebrating Passover with my family. But what could I do? I took the cross from his back and put it onto mine."

"Did you touch him, Abba?" Rufus asks.

Simon blinks. "I do not think so. I do not remember. All I remember is his face—pale and bloodied from a crown of thorns. He was in excruciating pain, but he took the time to look at me."

Simon pauses, the memory taking hold. "The centurion held a sign that read, 'This is the King of the Jews.'" At the time, he did not understand the significance of that statement, assumed it to be political mockery. Only when he heard the religious leaders taunting the man named Jesus did he understand the prisoner had upset not just Rome but the Sanhedrin as well.

"Women wailed and wept for him as we passed the gardens and went up to the Place of the Skull. The cross was heavy, but it was the suffering of the man in front of me and how he bore it that gave me strength to move forward beneath my own grief. I only had to make it to the execution site, and then I would be released."

"You did not see him upon the cross, then?" Rufus swats at a lock of hair on his brow.

Simon averts his gaze from his youngest child. How to make them understand? "I did not wish to see him suffer further. I had come to the city for a celebration. As soon as I gave the cross over, I sought the city gates. Had I known . . . had I understood . . . I hope I would have stayed and borne his sorrow with him."

Rachel touches Simon's arm. She understands. It is a small comfort.

"But that is not all, is it Abba?" Alexander says. "That is not the end."

Simon stops himself from turning away to hide the wetness creeping behind his eyes. "No, my son. That is not the end." He inhales a deep breath. "Several days later, I was walking to your uncle's house from the market. I saw a gathering of this man's disciples near the temple. I stopped to inquire of their excitement, and before the lot of us—I would say at least five hundred—the man whose cross I carried appeared, saying, 'Peace be with you.'"

Rufus stands. "It was him—wasn't it? Jesus the Lord?"

Simon's chest lightens. "Yes. He still had the marks upon his head, but now they shone. They were transformed with a beauty I did not comprehend. Not until we heard Peter talking that day during Shavuot. Not until the Ruach Hako'desh took up residence within me." He looks at each member of his family. "Within each of us.

"When I was carrying his cross, I did not understand what he was carrying of mine. Of ours. How the weight of that was more burdensome than any tree. And I abandoned him. I did not know. And yet, in his grace, he still came to me, both in flesh and in Spirit."

Rufus sniffs and throws his arms around Simon's neck. Simon inhales the scent of boy sweat and outdoor air. He holds his son to stare into his eyes. "I am honored to have carried that small weight of his burden, understand?" Simon looks to his other son. "He showed us what it is to love. In death, he showed us how to live." Simon gestures Alexander to him so the two boys are before him. "We must never forget what HaShem has done. And when we go through times of trouble, which we will, we must keep our eyes on him. He is never far. Do you understand, my boys?"

"We do, Abba!"

Simon draws Rachel to him and leans his head against her side. What would have happened if those Roman soldiers had never seized him that day? If he had not been late coming into the Holy City because of his father's death? Would he have heard of a risen prophet? Would he have cared? Would he have kept Peter and the other disciples in sight and watched their movement, strained to hear their words?

He has learned many things this past year, but one more comes to him now. Whatever door Adonai asks him to walk through, he will embrace it. For whatever the burden, whatever the suffering, the prize of drawing nearer to HaShem is worth the cost.

Reflection Questions

Read Matthew 5:38–42. Here, Jesus speaks about turning humiliation into action. How does he demonstrate this on his path to the cross? What does suffering as a follower of Jesus mean to you?

While there is no evidence that Simon of Cyrene became a believer, many scholars claim it significant that Mark would name Simon's sons, Alexander and Rufus, in his Gospel. Some even point out this could be the Rufus Paul names in the book of Romans. Imagine what growing up in a believing Simon's household might have been like.

Prayer

Heavenly Father, being here, on our way to the cross with you, is hard. It's hard to live it through words and remembering. And yet, Lord, it is through that remembering that we glimpse a deep part of your love. Thank you for that. Help us not be afraid to sit in pain and grief so that we might reach for the prize of drawing closer to you. Amen.

Suggested Reading

Mark 15:21–32

Acts 2:1–41

THIRTY-ONE

The Crucified Criminal

Inspired by Luke 23:32–43

As death creeps closer, the fear of God stirs within Dysmas, stoking to life memories and words from a forgotten childhood.

Hear, O Israel: the Lord is our God, the Lord is one.

While he has ignored such prayers in the past, the pain tearing through his body strips the last mental resistance from him. He pushes up with feet nailed to the wood of the tree to take a gasping breath. The movement aggravates his disjointed bones. It pulls at the nails driven into the tender skin and sinew of his hands, trailing a line of fire down his arms.

He breathes.

And as for you, you shall love the Lord your God with all your heart, with all your soul, and with all your strength.

"Abba, forgive them, for they do not know what they are doing."

Dysmas glances to his left at the Galilean man named Jesus. Dysmas does not understand the title placed above the man's execution stake, but it is apparent his death is not due to any great crime.

King of the Jews.

How is this "king" using the last of his breath to beseech forgiveness for those who placed him there? Those who even now cast lots for his clothes?

Members of the Sanhedrin stand nearby, as if to ensure that passersby understand the sign is meant as mockery. "He saved others; let him save himself if he is God's Messiah, the Chosen One."

Is Dysmas hallucinating? Would not the Jewish community, particularly members of the religious order, command silence and even pity in such a place of death?

But no. They have an ulterior motive, it seems. To make certain the sign above Jesus is not taken seriously.

In the hazy recesses of his mind, beyond the horrendous pain, Dysmas recalls stories of a Galilean rabbi said to make paralyzed men walk and blind men see. A teacher who raised a dead man from his grave, who unsettled the religious leaders. Many claim him as Messiah.

This, then, is that man. On his cross, between two common thieves.

For months, Dysmas and Chaim hid in the hills alongside the Jericho Road, making a living out of pilgrims foolish enough to travel alone. They stored away their stolen goods in the cave used by their band of revolutionaries.

Whatever passed on that road—money, clothes, animals, jewelry, food—was nothing a swift slingshot and a beating of a naive passerby could not earn.

Dysmas told himself he'd done what he must. He limited his victims to the well-off who prostituted themselves to the Romans, to the merchants from the Diaspora foolish enough to travel alone. He stole to stay alive, to support the zealots tucked away in the wilderness. Together, they would put an end to the unfair taxes and censuses that numbered his people like beasts at market.

Now, with flesh tearing from bone and the urgent need for breath, Dysmas wonders if it was worth it. Alongside this man whose only sin seems to be upsetting the religious leaders, Dysmas wonders how things might have been different.

Suffering alongside an upright man only makes him more aware of his stark transgressions. Would death be the expiation of his sins? Or would HaShem cast him away from the bosom of Israel forever?

Hear, O Israel: the Lord is our God, the Lord is one.

HaShem, forgive me, he prays.

It is fear that propels the prayer. He will never be able to prove the worth of his repentance. Will never be able to offer a sacrifice at the temple or try to find the men he hurt on the Jericho Road. He doubts HaShem will accept such a spindly, cowardly prayer, and yet it is all he has.

One of the soldiers offers him wine vinegar on a soaked rag, and Dysmas drinks, sucking the tart liquid from the dirtied cloth in hopes it will numb his pain.

The soldier moves to Jesus. "If you are the King of the Jews, save yourself."

Jesus does not answer.

On the other side of the Galilean, Chaim shouts. "Aren't you the Messiah? Save yourself and us!"

The sneer is meant to align himself with the soldiers. Perhaps Chaim will earn a quicker demise or something stronger than wine vinegar to ease his pain. But Dysmas cannot hang here and pretend he aligns himself with Chaim. Not any longer. Not here, on the brink of death with the would-be Messiah beside him.

He pushes up to gain breath and shouts at Chaim. "Don't you fear God, since you are under the same sentence?" A fresh stab of pain shoots down his back as splinters prick his spine. "We are punished justly, for we are getting what our deeds deserve. But this man has done nothing wrong." Dysmas looks at Jesus's bloodied face. Even now, it is impossible not to glimpse a holy shroud upon him.

This man is suffering on this cross for something only Dysmas deserves. "Jesus, remember me when you come into your kingdom."

Jesus winces as he pushes up on bloodied feet. "Truly I tell you, today you will be with me in paradise."

Paradise. The abode of the blessed.

Emotion washes over Dysmas. His body is broken, but his eyes are healed. He has been given a gift beyond measure—one of belief. He has been given a grace beyond measure—one of forgiveness. He has nothing to offer hanging from this cross, condemned as a prisoner. But Jesus accepts him anyway.

Against all odds, HaShem accepts him.

Dark clouds appear on the horizon as he thanks Jesus. He will suffer alongside him now. And though he does not yet know it, the events of the next few hours will only prove to increase the fledgling belief within him.

Reflection Questions

What was the difference between the two criminals crucified on either side of Jesus?

What part does repentance play in faith? As we near the time of Christ's death, take some time to practice this holy sacrament.

Prayer

Gracious Father, help us behold the extent of your grace and love. Thank you for your sacrifice that washes away the sins of the world. Forgive us, Lord, for our sins—known and unknown, things done and left undone. Help us put to rights what we can. Renew and purify our spirits. Amen.

Suggested Reading

Luke 23:32–43

THIRTY-TWO

The Death of a Son

Inspired by John 19:25–27

She cannot stand beneath the weight of grief that squeezes her spirit with iron-fisted hands.

Mary had known her heart would break in the end. But not like this. Seeing her beloved son beaten and bloodied upon that beam, his bones out of joint, thin strips of his rough woven tunic his only remaining covering, is more than she can bear.

Her legs give way. She barely registers the hands of her sister and sister-in-law. Somewhere close by she knows Aliza and John and Mary of Magdala are also here.

Fresh tears course down Mary's cheeks, and she bends over, emptying the contents of her stomach onto the dirt.

Adonai . . . no . . . it is too painful.

She remembers the words of the prophet Simeon the day she and Joseph brought Jesus to the temple as a baby. Words she has held close with a heady mixture of trepidation and acceptance.

This child is destined to cause the falling and rising of many in Israel, and to be a sign that will be spoken against, so that the thoughts of many hearts will be revealed. And a sword will pierce your own soul too.

She does not know what happened the night before, but she sees in the absence of Jesus's followers, in the mocking of the religious leaders, and even in the part the soldiers play in the death of her son, that the thoughts of many hearts have indeed been revealed. And she knows without a doubt a sword is piercing her soul, for she has never known such crushing pain.

If she could stop his agony—take it upon herself—she would. But this death is not hers to endure. Jesus was aware this would happen. Indeed, he intended it to happen.

It does not make it easier to bear.

All she can do is stand here, in crippling grief, and behold Jesus's suffering. Stand alongside him and embrace the sword piercing her own soul in an attempt to love her son as best she knows how.

She remembers him as a little boy hugging her when she most needed it—when the purse was empty of coins to feed a growing family, when James tried her patience, when Joseph lay frail in bed with fever.

It seems, in some ways, that Jesus has always been there with her. How will she bear losing him?

She does not fully understand Adonai's intentions, yet she knows Jesus is not surprised by this. Against all reason, she knows Adonai has a plan to redeem and restore all things, including her son's bruised and broken body.

And, despite the pain, if she'd known this would be how it ended, she would not have traded one hug with her little boy or one heart-to-heart moment with the man who is her son. She still would have said yes to the angel all those years ago.

She turns her face away from the soldiers at the base of the cross who cast lots for her son's clothing. She fights the urge to chastise and shame them, instead following Jesus's example.

There will be no more memories to make, and so she forces her gaze upon his face, etching every edge and corner into her mind, adding it to a thousand others she will cling to forevermore.

Jesus pushes up on his feet to draw breath. His glassy eyes stare down at her. "Woman."

He does not call her "Ima," and for that she is grateful. Hearing him call her "Mother" one last time may be her final undoing.

"Woman," he says again. "Here is your son." Jesus looks to John. "Here is your mother."

Her body convulses with sobs. Jesus is giving charge of her care not to his brothers, who have mocked his ministry, but to John, who has been one of his most faithful disciples. That Jesus is thinking of her well-being even when he suffers should not surprise her, but somehow it does.

John places an arm around her. Together, they pray. The hours wear on, the heaviest Mary has ever known. The sky grows dark. Jesus suffers on, and Mary stands by his feet, praying, wishing with all that is within her that she could help him bear his burden.

When the land grows dark as night, Jesus pushes up on his feet one last time. "Eloi, Eloi, lema sabachthani?"

My God, my God, why have you forsaken me?

Mary breathes around her pain. Her son cannot recite the entire psalm, but it is unmistakable he is implying the fullness of the verses to her, to the other women here, to John, to the religious leaders, to all who will listen.

Along with John, Aliza, Mary of Magdala, and Salome, she gives voice to the verses, ignoring the withering stares of the religious leaders. Mary senses Jesus is encouraged by King David's words, and that is enough for her.

> My God, my God, why have you forsaken me?
> Why are you so far from saving me,
> so far from my cries of anguish?
> My God, I cry out by day, but you do not answer,
> by night, but I find no rest.
>
> Yet you are enthroned as the Holy One;
> you are the one Israel praises.
> In you our ancestors put their trust;
> they trusted and you delivered them.
> To you they cried out and were saved;
> in you they trusted and were not put to shame.

Mary sinks into the ebb and flow of the verses. In many ways, they feel meant for this moment. She feels them with every fiber of her being. The words become part of her, infused into her heart as one infuses tea leaves in hot water.

> All the rich of the earth will feast and worship;
> all who go down to the dust will kneel before him—
> those who cannot keep themselves alive.
> Posterity will serve him;
> future generations will be told about the Lord.
> They will proclaim his righteousness,
> declaring to a people yet unborn:
> He has done it!

He has done it.

The words echo in Mary's heart, and although the piercing of her soul is fresh and festering, they serve as a small balm to help her glimpse a way forward, to anticipate what more Adonai will do.

Reflection Questions

Simply sit in the uncomfortable pain of this moment. What does it mean for Mary to stand alongside her suffering son?

Prayer

Heavenly Father, we offer to you our own prayers now, in word or in thought, thanking you for your faithfulness. Amen.

Suggested Reading

John 19:25–27
Psalm 22

THIRTY-THREE

The Hands That Pinned Him

Inspired by Luke 23:44–49

Longinus does not question orders. Crucifixion is never pleasant, but as a centurion in the Roman army, he does what he must to support his family, to carry out justice, and to honor Tiberius Caesar.

Another day on Golgotha should not bother him.

Why, then, when he drove the nails into the hands of the Galilean and raised him on the execution stake, did something unsettling niggle to the surface?

At first, he attempted to brush it aside. He had mocked the man alongside those in his charge, after all. He had looked on approvingly as they'd beaten and flogged him, plucked his beard, then wrapped a purple cloth around him and pushed a crown of thorns into his head, jeeringly paying homage to him.

I fear the army has taken away your humanity.

His wife's words echo in his head. It is their most recent argument, and he tires of it. When their small son, Marcus, runs and scuffs his knees, should he coddle him so he grows into a simpering milksop of a boy? There is only one way to make something of oneself in this world, and it is to be stronger than the next man.

Only, the Galilean does not appear strong. In fact, he did not fight back when they struck him but simply turned the other cheek—which, now that Longinus thinks about it, did serve as a sort of strength.

But the cry that had emanated from him when Longinus drove the long spikes into his hands and feet did not speak of strength. The words he'd echoed upon the cross, however, did.

Abba, forgive them, for they do not know what they are doing.

That made the hardened soldier uncomfortable. Longinus did not need forgiveness from the God of the Jews. He would've much preferred the criminal to spit upon him or beg for something to dull the pain.

The courageous presence of the Galilean's mother further served to prick at Longinus's raw spirit. She did not beg him to help her son. Neither did she plead with the Jewish leaders. She simply wept and prayed and stood alongside her child.

Longinus imagines Marcus grown and pinned to a Roman cross. Would it matter what crime he committed? Would Longinus not do everything he could to relieve his suffering?

He hopes the Galilean's demise will come swiftly.

The land grows eerily dark. Though it is midday, the soldiers light torches. Pilate, along with the religious leaders, is adamant that the man named Jesus be ensured dead before nightfall. A small storm will not deter Longinus from carrying out his duty.

Abba, forgive them, for they do not know what they are doing.

Truly I tell you, today you will be with me in paradise.

Woman, here is your son.

There is nothing that reveals the truth of a man like death. And as Longinus watches this man take death upon himself, he does not see Jesus in the light the Jewish leaders, or even Pilate, paint him in.

The Galilean appears . . . blameless.

Jesus cries out, and the women at the base of his cross take up one of their songs. The words pull at Longinus. They speak of a torturous plight and suffering, of the piercing of hands and feet, of bones poking through skin, of people staring and gloating. They speak of enemies casting lots for clothes.

The blood drains from Longinus's face. Does this old song . . . speak of this man? Of events that have transpired because of *him*? Is such a thing possible?

Longinus's limbs tremble. He is grateful for the darkness so his subordinates will not witness his terror.

"I thirst," the man named Jesus says.

Longinus fills a sponge with the rough wine of the soldiers and fastens it to the stalk of a hyssop plant. The Galilean drinks.

When he turns his face away, Longinus lowers the stalk.

"It is finished," Jesus cries out. "Abba, into your hands I commit my spirit." He inhales a small, rattling breath.

And then, all is silent.

Longinus stares at the now-still body of the Galilean. The sky lightens. What does it mean to commit one's spirit to a heavenly Father?

He falls to his knees, knowing with sudden certainty that they have made a horrible mistake. "Surely this was a righteous man. God of this Galilean, forgive me."

He does not care that his soldiers see. All he can focus on is the piercing guilt that crushes his soul.

The next three days are dark. Longinus helps seal Jesus's tomb. He goes home and hugs his son. He wakes at night beside his wife to find foreign tears on his pillow. He makes sacrifices to Mars.

But it's not until he holds the unbroken Roman seal in his hand and sees the frayed edges of the burst ropes at the tomb three days later that he begins to question the truth. It's not until years later, when Longinus sits in his friend Cornelius's house and listens to a man named Peter explain the mysteries of that long-ago day, that a holy fire of belief comes upon him.

He is baptized that very day beside Cornelius's home. And when he comes up out of the water, Longinus is a new man.

Reflection Questions

What forces are pulling at Longinus during the crucifixion? What forces pull at you? Which are worthy and which are not?

Imagine how the centurion at the cross felt to hear Jesus utter the words, "Father, forgive them, for they do not know what they are doing."

Prayer

Father, you took upon yourself not just our sin but our guilt and our shame. Thank you for your love and your amazing grace. May we seek to place our spirits in your hands every minute of every day.

Suggested Reading

Luke 23:44–49

THIRTY-FOUR

Secret Disciple

Inspired by John 19:31–42

Joseph's heart takes up a fierce beating as he hastens alongside Nicodemus to Pilate's residence. There is no turning back. In fact, he *must* do this. He must honor his Lord in death. He may have succumbed to fear before, but Jesus's body will not be left to beasts of prey. His Lord must have a proper burial.

Beyond gilded doors, they enter the throne room chambers of the praetorium. Pilate sits atop ornamental pillows and sips from a golden cup. When Joseph and Nicodemus bow before the governor, he smiles. "I have never had so many esteemed Sanhedrinists visit me in one day. What can I do for you?"

Joseph steps forward. His long robes and noble carriage speak of wealth, and he hopes the governor will look favorably upon him. "We wish to request custody of the body of Jesus of Nazareth, who has been crucified on Golgotha." His voice does not betray the quaking within.

Pilate raises a slim eyebrow. "He is dead already?"

"He is, governor," Joseph says.

Pilate claps his hands, and a servant appears. "Fetch me Longinus. And be quick about it."

"Yes, sir."

Pilate addresses Joseph and Nicodemus. "You may wait in the antechamber."

Joseph watches the shadows grow long from the window of Pilate's marble-clad antechamber. He thinks of Jesus's last words. *It is finished.* He thinks of the weeping mother, of the rumor he heard in the streets of the temple curtain being rent in two. Has the entire world turned upside down this day?

When the centurion from Golgotha finally enters, Joseph stands, but Pilate's servants block him from approaching the throne room.

After a few moments, Longinus exits. Joseph and Nicodemus are summoned.

"Please," Joseph says to the centurion before he departs. "Do not dispose of the body. I wish to bury him properly."

The centurion lowers his gaze to the Persian rug of the antechamber. "I will hold it until sundown."

Sundown, the beginning of the High Sabbath—a most holy day that includes the second day of Passover and Shabbat. Jesus's body must be prepared and buried before the first three stars appear in the sky. They must hurry.

"Thank you."

"Where will you take the body?" Pilate asks when they stand before him once again.

"There is a new tomb nearby, one I have commissioned be hewn for my family. We will lay him there," Joseph says.

Pilate nods. "Very well. My servant will send you with a letter." He dismisses them, mumbling something about the odd ways of the Jews.

After a few more minutes of waiting to receive the letter with Pilate's seal, they hasten out of the city and toward Golgotha. Nicodemus's servants, carrying nearly seventy-five pounds of myrrh, aloes, and clean linen strips, follow behind. They arrive to see one of the soldiers dragging the criminal on the left of Jesus away from the cross.

Joseph hands the centurion the letter. "We are to take his body."

The centurion nods. Joseph turns to the cross but glimpses the crumpled form of Jesus's mother. This will not be pleasant.

"I will lay him in my family tomb, in the garden across the way," he says to the one remaining disciple. "You have my word." It is of utmost importance that this man, little more than a youth, believe him.

"Thank you," the man whispers. He coaxes Jesus's mother to follow him away from the cross and, after some resistance, she does.

"Should I call for more servants?" Nicodemus asks.

Joseph looks up at the battered, dirty body of the man he admired—the man he did not do more to save. "No. I will do it."

He removes his mantle and rolls a hefty rock closer to the cross to better reach Jesus's body. The centurion, surprisingly gentle with the body, assists with the spikes. When the heavy weight falls into Joseph's arms, he is overcome with emotion.

What have they done to this holy one of HaShem?

By the time they reach the rock-hewn tomb, Joseph is sweating and his arms tremble with the weight. He lays Jesus tenderly on a patch of grass and enlists the help of Nicodemus's servants and two nearby gardeners to roll away the great circular stone in front of the tomb.

Once they accomplish the feat, Joseph lays Jesus upon the cold entrance. The cavern echoes with their movements. Nicodemus's servants fetch water and light candles by which to wash and tend the body.

Joseph does not hide his tears as he and Nicodemus remove broken pieces of thorns from Jesus's head. They wipe blood and sweat from his plucked beard and matted hair. With gentleness, they turn the body to clean out the deep lashes of a Roman flogging. They pick out the many splinters and pieces of lead riddling his wounds. His hands and feet are shattered, and a cavernous wound gapes open on his side.

They work quickly, but night falls fast. The first thin call of the shofar signaling the beginning of Shabbat meets them within the tomb.

"You will not allow your Holy One to see decay," Nicodemus whispers as they smooth the myrrh and aloe upon Jesus's body and wrap one limb at a time with the clean cloth. Joseph thinks he will never smell the pungent, earthy spices again without being carried back to this moment.

As the sun dips below the horizon, they say a final prayer and leave an excess of spices alongside the body before heaving the stone in front of the garden-tomb once more.

Joseph returns home with a heavy heart as the final call of the ram's horn sounds. Six ritual trumpet blasts follow, announcing the Sabbath day of the Passover, holy above all others. Inside homes, Shabbat lamps are lit. A blanket of quiet reverence falls over the city.

He acknowledges a deeper understanding of himself, of what it means to be close to death, of what it means to realize his failures but seek redemption nonetheless. The trials of this day have fanned something to life that burns bright within him.

Today, he is no longer a secret disciple. Today, he is no longer ashamed of Jesus. Today, a part of him has been buried with his Lord.

Reflection Questions

What do you think stopped Joseph of Arimathea and Nicodemus from admitting they were disciples before Jesus's death?

How do you think ministering to the body of Jesus changed them forever?

Prayer

Heavenly Father, as we look back in history at all you orchestrated around your Passion, we are thankful at the same time we are saddened. May we feel a healthy amount of guilt, may we mourn as those with hope, and may we await your new kingdom as we enter into good works that bring your dominion to earth even now. Amen.

Suggested Reading

John 19:31–42
Matthew 27:57–61
Psalm 16

THIRTY-FIVE

The Guard's Bribe

Inspired by Matthew 27:62–28:15

Noam watches his commander Longinus position the seal over the thick ropes he and Spurius finished securing over the large stone of the tomb.

Ridiculous, all the fuss the religious leaders are making over the dead Galilean.

And yet only a powerful man could have caused such alarm to run rampant through the city's elite. And there had been much alarm. From Herod to Pilate to the chief priest and the Sanhedrin—and all during one of the Jews' most holy feast weeks.

Not to mention the reports of the soldiers who returned to the fortress last night from Golgotha. They told strange stories—of the sky growing dark, of an earthquake Noam had not felt, of the Galilean forgiving those who hammered the stakes and promising new life to the criminal on his right.

Strange happenings, indeed.

Longinus turns to the chief priests and teachers looking on with folded arms. "That is as secure as I know how to make it. Would you like to inspect?"

One in the front inches toward the tomb, the prayer tassels of his long garment almost sweeping the ground. "Someone could still cut away the seal and the rope to steal the body."

The dead Galilean promised to rise after three days. These men fear his disciples will steal away his body and tell others he has been raised. But what respectable Jewish man would contaminate himself with a rotting corpse?

Noam wipes the sweat from his brow. He does not care about these people's religious quarrels. He does not understand them. Who in their right mind would worship a single God with no image? He only cares about serving Pilate, about making a name for himself in the Roman army.

Longinus releases a deep sigh. "May your God help whoever dares to break a Roman imperial seal. If it is damaged, you know someone broke into the tomb. Is that not the evidence you need?"

The leader nods, mouth firm above his long oiled beard. "I insist on two guards."

"You may have them." Longinus turns to Noam and Spurius. "You will remain here until I send someone to relieve you. I will send food and supplies."

Noam bites back a complaint. Guard duty is among the dullest work of a soldier. When will he see battle and earn honor? Even supervising on Golgotha would be of more import than guarding a tomb in a peaceful garden.

Longinus starts back to the city gates with the religious leaders, leaving Noam and Spurius alone in front of the tomb.

Spurius seeks a spot beneath a fig tree and sits beside his pack. "What's it going to be, then? Tali or terni lapilli?"

Noam is sick of games. He wants power. He wants blood.

He swigs a flask of posca, its tart flavor washing down his throat. "Longinus sympathizes with this dead Galilean."

Spurius shrugs. "What is that to us?"

"Just an observation," Noam mutters.

The day wears on. The garden is quiet, peaceful even. Noam hates it. Later that night, a soldier brings food and drink.

Noam sleeps while Spurius takes the first watch, but he wakes in the middle of the night to see, by the light of the moon, that his companion has also fallen asleep. He punches his comrade hard in the gut.

Spurius wakes, sputtering. "What was that for?"

"You fell asleep!"

"You imbecile! No one is going to touch a Roman seal. This place is the most dismal post. What are you anxious about?"

"I am not anxious. I take my job for the governor seriously," Noam growls.

"I'll stay awake the rest of the night, then. I won't even sit. You can have all the beauty sleep to yourself."

"No. *I'll* take my intended shift, and *I* will stay awake."

"Suit yourself." Spurius readjusts his pack against the fig tree.

Noam is true to his word. After inspecting the rope and the seal and seeing it intact, he walks the length of the path in front of the tomb to keep himself awake. He grumbles about Spurius's work ethic. He grumbles about Longinus's orders to place him in such a lowly post. He grumbles about his commander's slowness to promote him.

As hazy pink streaks lighten the eastern sky, Noam stifles a yawn. Now that daylight breaks, perhaps Spurius can be trusted to take a shift and allow him some sleep.

He kicks Spurius's boot.

Without warning, the earth shakes violently, upending Noam off his feet and casting him to the ground. The brightest of lights, as bright as lightning, fringe the cracks between the stone and the tomb. Noam shields his eyes but sees a figure in pure white rolling back the stone. The ropes burst. The seal falls to the ground.

Noam's limbs tremble. What sort of a being is this? Black pinpricks drift before his eyes. The last thing he remembers is the ground coming up to meet him.

When he wakes, the sun peers just over the horizon. The garden is quiet. A pair of white doves fly above. Did he fall asleep? What a tremendous nightmare. He ignores his aching head and pushes himself onto an elbow.

He looks at the tomb.

Terror clamps around his throat. It is not possible.

He scurries to his feet. "Spurius, wake!"

Noam inspects the ropes, frayed as though pulled with inconceivable force. He picks up the seal on the ground, whole and intact. He drops it.

Most unbelievable is the fact that the stone is rolled away.

His heart beats so fast he fears he might faint again. The memory of the great heavenly being grips him.

It was not a dream.

"What happened?" Spurius staggers to his feet.

"You saw it too, didn't you? Didn't you?"

"I was sleeping. It was your watch."

Noam restrains himself from slapping Spurius upside the head. "You could not have slept through that earthquake."

Spurius reddens. "I do seem to remember a tremble," he admits.

Noam points to the unbroken seal and Spurius's eyes widen.

"Impossible."

"Go see if the body is there."

"The Jews would have a conniption if Gentiles enter their burial place. You go, if you're so curious."

Noam grits his teeth and enters the tomb. The scents of myrrh and aloe mix with the earthy smells of the underground. He does not see a wrapped body in the left compartment or straight ahead. He peers into the right chamber and stops at the sight of linen cloths separate from a head napkin, all folded as if the body had just slipped from them.

He backs out of the tomb, limbs vibrating, skin crawling.

"Have you seen a ghost?" Spurius asks.

"The body is gone."

"Impossible." Despite his earlier objection, Spurius enters the tomb. When he exits, his face is pale. "We must report this to the governor."

"Are you serious? He will have our heads."

"What will we do?"

Noam's mind spins. "We will go to the chief priests and religious leaders. They have Pilate's ear. They knew something like this would happen—that is why they were adamant about securing the tomb."

When they reach the temple and gain an audience with three religious leaders in a chamber outside the hall of polished stones, Noam shows them the unbroken seal.

"The ropes are frayed, but not as if they were cut," Noam reports. "The body is gone."

They stare at him, their eyebrows furrowed.

"That is not all."

"Go on then, man," a Pharisee prods.

"There was a . . . being. A bright being. I saw him roll away the stone."

The Pharisee sways. "Wait here. We will be back."

When they return, they hand a large bag of money to Noam. The weight of it feels like power.

"This is what you will say to your commanding officers. Tell them that his disciples came and stole him away at night while you were asleep."

"I never fall asleep on duty," Noam sneers.

"It is the only way. If this report gets to the governor, we will satisfy him and keep you out of trouble."

Noam feels the weight of the money in his hands. He remembers that terrifying being bursting the ropes on that tomb. He glances at Spurius, who nods.

What other choice do they have?

"We will do as you say."

Reflection Questions

Matthew records that the guards saw the angel of the Lord. What do you think played into their decision to disregard this sighting or write it off as an illusion? How do you think they might have explained away what they saw?

When are you tempted to cling to preconceived notions instead of sitting in the uncomfortable gray of an issue? How can we be mindful of guarding against this as we move forward in our faith?

Prayer

Lord, grant us wisdom to discern what is of true worth in this world and in this life. May we see the allure of power and success and wealth as rubbish compared to the offer of your kingdom and your grace. Open our eyes to your glory. Amen.

Suggested Reading

Matthew 27:62–28:15

THIRTY-SIX

The First to See

Inspired by John 20:1–18 and Luke 24:1–12

It is still dark when Mary wakes.

In some ways, she wonders if her soul will ever see light again.

"Joanna." She feels around for the bag of spices Nicodemus gifted her.

"I am awake." The movement of Joanna's straw pallet beside hers sounds in the quiet. More soft, female voices echo in the room.

In short order, they start for the garden. The several women are quiet, used to one another's company after so many months of traveling together, learning together, serving together. Now, grief hangs over them like a thick cloak on a hot day, but love thrusts them forward to perform this last act for their teacher. Their friend. Their Lord.

Their wounded hope.

Mary blinks away tears as they approach the garden. She tries to block out the memory of three days earlier, but it sneaks in like a demon in the night. She cannot see anything besides the image of her beloved Jesus bloodied and bruised and broken on the cross. A sob slips out. James's mother tucks an arm around her shoulders.

The faintest hint of peachy light climbs the eastern horizon, and Mary concentrates on the mission before them. Will they be able to roll the stone away? But of course they will. She could accomplish the task herself with the mere determination of her love.

As they approach the place where they saw Nicodemus and Joseph lay their rabbi, Mary wipes away her tears. Enough. They have important work to do.

She focuses on the abundant purple and saffron crocuses to the side of the path. When she looks up, she stops short and gasps.

The other women follow her gaze. Their sounds of surprise confirm she is not seeing things.

The great stone is rolled from the entrance.

Giant heaves work through Mary's chest. She remembers the horrible things done to Jesus. Could they not allow him to rest in death?

"They have disturbed him and taken his body so he will not have a proper burial." Joanna clutches the jar of perfume in her hands.

Mary's grief mounts as she imagines thieves desecrating her Savior's body. Her stomach roils. She breathes deep, willing her nausea to pass.

"We must tell the others," James's mother says.

Mary hands the bag of spices to Joanna. "I will go." She is the youngest. She can run to Peter and John's lodgings faster than the others.

As she runs, her tears flow. She remembers the life she knew in Magdala before Jesus. The torment of the demons. Seven of them—one causing paralysis, another causing hearing loss, still another tempting her to harm herself. The slew of others attacked her mind, darkening her days, robbing her of normal life.

She still loathes the dark.

But Jesus caused light to flood in. With one touch, the demons fled. She was healed. Jesus gave her purpose. He invited her into the law. Into his kingdom. He encouraged her to share it. He gave her hope.

How can life without him be worth living?

Chest heaving, she bangs on the door of the home where Peter and John stay. Tears streak her face, but she cares little. Peter opens the door, his eyes hollow and heavy with grief.

He has lost his hope too.

"Come quickly. They have taken the Lord out of the tomb, and we don't know where they have put him!"

Peter's face pales. He calls back to John. In moments, they race from the house. John, the younger of the pair, pulls ahead of Peter before they reach the end of the street.

The women have likely returned to their lodgings, but what good will Mary be there? She must see what Peter and John make of the stone being rolled away.

She forces her legs forward, stumbling. When she finally reaches the garden, rosy fingers of sunlight reach into the sky. There is no sign of Peter or John or the other women. Have they sought answers elsewhere?

The distant thundering of bronze indicates the Nicanor Gate of the temple is being opened. The sound of trumpets announcing the first prayer meets her ears and she recites the Shema through her tears as she reaches the tomb.

With the words complete, she peers inside the hewn rock to the stone bench to the right, where Nicodemus and Joseph worked before Shabbat. She blinks. The graveclothes lie neatly on the bench, hardened with the aloes and spices. But there is no body within them. How could the robbers remove the body so neatly from the cloths?

None of it makes sense. More warm tears wet her raw cheeks.

Without warning, two men in blinding white appear near the graveclothes, one at the head and the other at the feet.

"Woman, why are you crying?"

Another racking sob escapes her body. Immeasurable grief shrouds her mind. Who are these men? She hardly cares. "They have taken my Lord away and I don't know where they have put him."

How can she prepare his body for burial if she does not know where the body is?

She turns from the darkness of the tomb and sees another man at its entrance. Bursting dawn sparkles behind him, and while the form of his shadow looks familiar, she cannot place where she has seen him. Perhaps here in the garden, when Nicodemus and Joseph prepared Jesus's body?

"Woman," he says. "Why are you crying? Who are you looking for?"

Is he the gardener, then? "Sir, if you have carried him away, tell me where you have put him, and I will get him."

She does not care that she is but a single woman. She *will* perform this last act of love for her Lord.

"Mary."

She gasps, closes her eyes.

Mary. Like an entire message in one word, meant only for her.

The sound of her name opens a well of understanding deep in her spirit. She *does* know that voice.

She remembers the touch that freed her from the demons. The name he spoke—a name that no longer binds her with curse, but with life.

It *is* him.

"Rabboni!" She falls to his feet, clasping his ankles, clinging fiercely to him. His skin is solid and warm beneath her fingers. His feet are still pierced, but they do not call to mind the ugliness of a few days ago, only an unusual beauty.

He is *here*. He is alive and breathing. Never again will she release him.

Many moments pass before he speaks gently. "Mary, you must stop clinging to me. I have not yet ascended to the Father. Go instead to my brothers and tell them, 'I am ascending to my Father and your Father, to my God and your God.'"

She does not understand his words, but one thing is clear. He is flesh and bone. He is different, but the same. He is *alive*.

With tears in her eyes and with the sun shining brilliantly above, she runs again. But this time, she flies as if on the wings of eagles. She does not grow weary, for the sight of her risen Savior propels her forward. She can hardly wait to tell the others.

Their Lord is alive!

She bursts into the lodgings of Peter and John to find them sitting at their table, looks of puzzled distress upon their faces. But all is better now.

Their hope lives.

"I have seen the Lord!"

Reflection Questions

Read Exodus 25:22. Consider the placement of the angels at the head and feet of Jesus's graveclothes. Contrast this with the placement of the cherubim on the mercy seat (the place where the high priest sprinkled the blood offering for the atonement of the Lord's people). What is the significance of this?

When Eve's eyes were opened in the garden of Eden, she hid from shame. In this story, Mary's eyes are opened when Jesus calls her name. He then invites her into the work of proclaiming the Good News, even before the men. How does this moment of resurrection speak of the renewal of creation?

Prayer

Holy Father, you mend broken things, you restore us to who we were meant to be in that beautiful garden. Help us do the faithful work of chasing after you, of joyfully carrying out your good works, and of sharing your love with those around us. Amen.

Suggested Reading

John 20:1–18
Luke 24:1–12

THIRTY-SEVEN

The Emmaus Road

Inspired by Luke 24:13-34

Mary walks beside her husband, Cleopas, as they leave Yerushalayim through the Western Gate. Pilgrims still crowd the Holy City for the Passover celebration, but she and her husband long to travel the sixty furlongs home to Emmaus.

The last few days have turned their lives upside down.

Silence envelops the pair as they voyage the first stretch of road. Not until they reach the brink of the plateau, their blood-soaked, beloved city behind them, does Mary finally speak.

"I wish I had gone with them this morning." The women had come back from Jesus's grave with amazing news. If only she had seen for herself!

Cleopas squeezes her arm. Always kind, age has softened and polished him to a lustrous gold. She is proud to call him her husband and the father of their grown children. Prouder still that, when their eldest son came to him with news of a rabbi from Galilee, Cleopas did not allow pride to hinder him in seeking out the man of Adonai.

"You are much help to Abilene. Being a grandfather is wonderful, but that babe would have kept us up through the night."

Mary remembers the feel of her grandson settled against her in the wee hours of the morning. She had been up half the night with him. If only . . .

"I meant to wake earlier. If I had known . . ." She lets the words trail off and breathes in the fresh air, no longer tainted by the stench of sacrifices and the memories of the last few days.

They pass the next stretch of road. They enter a valley where Bethlehem is nestled in the far-off distance. They walk with no words for a long while until she cannot hold back any longer. "Do you think it could be true? Do you think he could be . . . alive?"

Perhaps if she had seen the angels herself . . .

Cleopas does not answer right away. "We had so much hope. I, too, wonder if another hope is possible."

"Another hope?" They leave the well-paved Roman road and head up the path to their hometown of Emmaus.

"Peter and John said the grave linens were not cut away. How does one remove all the cloths without cutting them?"

Mary shakes her head as they climb the hill. She knows from experience how quickly spices and aloes harden linen in the cool of a tomb.

Without warning, another man walks alongside them. She chastises herself for being so enraptured with her thoughts as to be oblivious to the man coming up behind them.

They must be careful.

"Shalom," the man says.

"Shalom," they return, continuing up the path.

"You are deep in conversation. Do not let me stop you. Tell me, what are you discussing as you walk along?"

When Cleopas stops, Mary does also. How can this stranger be unaware of such happenings? Tears gather beneath her eyelids at the thought of having to hear her husband recount the events of three days ago.

Cleopas gestures back to the Holy City. "Are you the only one visiting Yerushalayim who does not know the things that have happened there in these days?"

"What things?" the stranger asks.

"About Jesus of Nazareth," Cleopas says. "He was a prophet powerful in word and deed before God and all the people."

The passion in Cleopas's voice is apparent. No stranger could be fooled into thinking her husband did not love this prophet. And although sadness and secrecy shrouded the dispersed followers since that horrid day of Jesus's crucifixion, now Mary is proud of her husband for sharing about their teacher. What's more, a sudden burning within her tells her it is right to share.

Cleopas bites his lip. "The chief priests and our rulers handed him over to be sentenced to death, and they crucified him; but we had hoped that he was the one who was going to redeem Israel."

Redeem Israel. What would a new kingdom ruled by Jesus have looked like?

The threesome move farther into the region of hills. A stream babbles beside them. The scents of lemons and oranges waft from the nooks. All seems brighter here as they walk toward their home beside this stranger.

"And what is more, it is the third day since all this took place. In addition, some of our women amazed us."

Cleopas stops to gather his breath, but Mary rushes on to finish her husband's sentence. "They went to the tomb early this morning but didn't find his body! They came and told us they had seen a vision of angels, who said he was alive."

Cleopas nods. "Then some of our companions went to the tomb and found it just as the women had said, but they did not see Jesus."

They wait for the stranger to comprehend their words, but instead he shakes his head in a somehow familiar manner. "How foolish you are, and how slow to believe all that the prophets have spoken! Did not the Messiah have to suffer these things and then enter his glory?"

Mary cannot untangle the myriad emotions the stranger's words elicit within her. First, that he understands them. Second, that he calls their Lord the *Messiah*.

Is that not what they believed and hoped all this time? That Jesus would be the one to save them?

As they pass olive groves and fruit trees, the stranger teaches them. Mary feels like a small girl learning the Torah all over again at her father's knee. He speaks of the faith of Abel and Enoch and Noah and Abraham and Moses. He speaks of the lamb's blood spread over the Israelites' doors before the exodus from Egypt. He speaks of King David and the prophets. Isaiah and Joel, Jeremiah and Malachi.

By the time they approach their village, Mary is in a glorious whirlwind. Satiation and longing perform a dance within her burning heart. Her husband's face glows.

"Sir, you have given us confidence again. We understand now that Jesus is the Christ—how did we not see it before?"

They pause at the city gates, but the stranger moves ahead.

"Stay with us!" Cleopas calls. "It's nearly evening, and the day is almost over."

The man agrees. They lead him to their house, where Mary prepares a quick meal of leftover unleavened bread, figs, and lentils. Cleopas asks their guest to honor them with the blessing.

He takes the bread and lifts it. "Blessed are you, O Lord our God, King of the universe, who brings forth bread from the earth." He breaks the bread and offers them each a piece.

Mary's hand flies to her chest.

It is *him*.

It is their Lord!

How did she not see what is so undeniable?

But then he is gone.

She turns to Cleopas. "It was Jesus!"

"As soon as he offered the broken bread, I understood!" her husband exclaims. "But how did we not recognize him?"

"Were not our hearts burning within us while he talked to us on the road and opened the Scriptures to us?"

"We must return to Yerushalayim right away."

Mary grins. No matter that it grows dark, she can think of nothing she would rather do. For there is no longer any reason to fear and every reason to gather with Jesus's disciples and share this most glorious news.

Reflection Questions

Consider how close these two disciples were to Jesus while not being aware of his presence. In what ways does busyness and unbelief prevent us from seeing our Savior?

After they reached Emmaus, Jesus seems to be continuing on, but verse 29 says "they urged him strongly" or "constrained him" to stay. Meditate on how your longing and love for Jesus might constrain him to be a part of your own life.

Prayer

All-powerful God, in our seeking of you may we better glimpse your face. In the glimpsing of your face and of who you are, may we more easily release the things of this world that tempt us to grasp inconsequential things. Remind us of who we are in you. Amen.

Suggested Reading

Luke 24:13–35

THIRTY-EIGHT

The Shore of Redemption

Inspired by John 21:1–25

The night unfurls like a dark blanket over the Galilean Sea. If Peter imagines hard enough, he can remember a night much like this one—the night before his life changed forever.

If he could do it over again, he would do better. He would be wiser, make different choices.

And yet, if he is learning one thing, it is that though he is apt to fail—and will fail—his Lord will not.

Praise HaShem.

With the help of his brother Andrew and several of the other disciples, including James and John, they haul in their net. Sand clogs the holes. Pebbles have torn it in spots.

"I seem to recall there being fish in this lake," Andrew jokes.

"Much has changed." Peter thinks of his wife, Naamah. He must tell her all that transpired last Paschal week before she hears it from others.

They again throw out their nets. Maybe they are not meant to be fishermen any longer. Maybe Leviathan stalks them on these open waters. But Jesus told them to return to Galilee. The scandal of their crucified rabbi dried up their support. Should they not go back to what they know to support their families?

And yet . . . Jesus is alive. That is all that matters. Peter has seen him with his own eyes. He is the same Jesus he always knew, and yet he is more. He is bright and whole, shining and complete.

Peter blinks back tears of gratitude and something else—a piercing guilt that niggles him.

The rosy hue of daybreak touches the horizon, illuminating a figure on shore. "Friends," the figure calls. "Haven't you any fish?"

A common enough greeting among working men, but not one Peter wishes to answer with an empty net in hand. The others answer with resounding noes.

The man on shore points to the opposite side of their boat. "Throw your net on the right side of your boat and you will find some."

Peter squints at the man but sees only a shadowy figure through the morning mist. The others look to Peter. He shrugs. What can it hurt? They throw the net on the right side of the boat.

It sinks to the bottom. A moment later, the boat tilts to the right. Peter blinks, grasping for the net with the others.

It is heavy. So heavy. Peter looks at the stranger. How . . . ? They pull at the nets. Such a shoal of fish they have struck!

The corners of Peter's eyes grow wet at the remembrance of that day he first left his net to follow Jesus.

Go away from me, Lord, for I am a sinful man!

Don't be afraid; from now on you will fish for people.

John slaps Peter on the arm. "It is the Lord!"

The truth hits hard—much like this weight of fish they drag. John is right. It is Jesus!

Without hesitating, Peter scoops up his mantle and wraps it around himself before plunging into the water. This time, he will reach Jesus first.

As he swims the two hundred cubits to shore, he remembers walking on these very same waters toward Jesus. He remembers sinking, grasping for his hand.

Emotion lodges in his throat. He climbs the pebbly shore, his wet mantle clinging to his legs. The boat comes behind him. The scent of a coal-burning fire wafts through the air. It stings his eyes and brings with it memories of another fire, this one at a charcoal brazier in the courtyard of the high priest.

You aren't one of this man's disciples too, are you?

Peter clears his throat as he sees Jesus has laid fish on the fire. Why should he be surprised that their Lord has already provided everything they need in such a humble manner?

Lord, are you going to wash my feet?

You do not realize now what I am doing, but later you will understand.

If he had not fallen asleep in Gethsemane, if he had prayed as Jesus instructed, would he have failed so horribly? Would he have drawn his sword? Would he have fled, then thought himself brave to follow Jesus into the high priest's home?

Lord, why can't I follow you now? I will lay down my life for you.

Will you really lay down your life for me? Very truly I tell you, before the rooster crows, you will disown me three times.

Such bravery, to deny his Lord three times while they plucked his rabbi's beard and taunted him to prophesy.

"Bring some of the fish you have just caught," Jesus instructs.

There is already enough on the coals, but Peter obeys, going back to the boat and hauling the massive catch to shore. He selects a few of the fish while noting there is not one unclean among them. Not one! He adds the work of their hands to Jesus's already generous table.

They eat together.

Peter marvels at the humanness of his rabbi, his Lord. Yet something gleams as well, reminding Peter of how Jesus looked on Mount Tabor. His face glows. He heralds good will.

"Peace be with you," Jesus had said when he'd appeared to them in Yerushalayim.

And that is what Peter knows now, in his presence: peace.

After only charred fish bones and coals remain, Jesus turns to Peter. "Simon ben John, do you love me more than these?"

Peter swallows, the use of his old name like bitter herbs on the tongue of his Lord. He has not been a rock. He has not earned the name of Peter.

Even if all fall away on account of you, I never will.

He is a wretched man.

But no longer. Peter straightens, determined to answer correctly, to prove his devotion once and for all. "Yes, Lord. You know that I love you."

"Feed my lambs." Jesus's eyes shine. "Simon ben John, do you love me?"

Peter's heart sinks. Does Jesus not believe him? "Yes, Lord. You know that I love you."

"Take care of my sheep."

I am the good shepherd. The good shepherd lays down his life for the sheep.

"Simon ben John, do you love me?"

Defeat wells within Peter at Jesus asking him a third time, a ringing reminder of the three times he denied his rabbi in the courtyard of the high priest. "Lord, you know all things; you know that I love you."

Could his Lord not see his sincerity, his heart? Or was this for the sake of the others?

Jesus's eyes soften, and Peter's chest drains of pressure.

"Very truly I tell you, when you were younger you dressed yourself and went where you wanted; but when you are old you will stretch out your hands, and someone else will dress you and lead you where you do not want to go. Follow me!"

Peter nods. He will do whatever Jesus asks of him. In the light of his love, nothing else matters.

Still, his gaze drifts to John. "Lord, what about him?"

He and John have often found themselves competing for the spot closest to their teacher. Was John to be a shepherd too? Was he to find an end such as Peter's?

"If I want him to remain alive until I return, what is that to you?"

Peter bites his lip. Whatever path his Lord has for him, he will walk it. Even if it is different from John's.

In the end, it does not matter, and perhaps someday he will learn that.

All that matters is his love for the Savior who continues to pull him up from the threat of dark waters.

Reflection Questions

Many times throughout his ministry, Jesus challenges what Peter believes to be of most importance. Take a moment to honestly examine your priorities. Have a conversation with God surrounding what you discover.

In this story, Jesus commissions Peter to sustain his brothers and guide the new church. After the arrival of the Holy Spirit at Pentecost, we see an emboldened, new Peter who eventually dies willingly for the sake of the gospel. What does this say about the role of the Holy Spirit in our lives?

Prayer

Heavenly Father, thank you for challenging us to love as you love. Help us keep our eyes fixed on you and not on the race of those running beside us. May your Holy Spirit take up residence within us this day and forevermore. Amen.

Suggested Reading

John 21:1–25

Acts 2:14–41

THIRTY-NINE

Determined Brother

Inspired by the Book of Jude

Jude's calamus travels over parchment, scraping along with satisfying speed. The words flow free, and he does not question them.

But you, dear friends, by building yourselves up in your most holy faith and praying in the Holy Spirit, keep yourselves in God's love as you wait for the mercy of our Lord Jesus Christ to bring you to eternal life.

He rubs cramped fingers, thick with arthritis. His mind travels to a time when his hands and bones did not ache, when he was barely in his third decade. His gaze falls to the parchment.

Wait for the mercy of our Lord Jesus Christ.

He closes his eyes.

Jesus.

After many years of humbling experience, he is proud to know Jesus as his Master and Lord. But sometimes . . . sometimes, he allows himself to remember Jesus as the brother of his youth. The brother who taught him to bang hammer on nails, the brother who gave rides atop his shoulders when Jude was on the brink of frustration for being so small. The brother whom he sometimes resented for being so annoyingly perfect in every way.

Forgive me, Father. Jude remembers trudging down the dusty road to Capernaum from Nazareth two years before Jesus's death. The sure steps of his brothers James and Joses in front of him, Aliza and Mary a few paces behind with their mother.

The night before, James told them news of the unseemly crowd Jesus attracted. His brother had sat at the table after washing his feet in the vessel of water at the door. "He's making a spectacle of himself."

The lines around their mother's mouth deepened. "Jesus knows what he's doing."

But her voice lacked surety.

When Joses came into the house from the workshop, he agreed with James's suggestion that they leave in the morning to bring Jesus home. "One of my customers told me Jesus is doing wild things, that he is belligerent with the teachers of the law."

Fear for his older brother consumed Jude. Surely, Jesus wouldn't be giving the teachers trouble. What kind of false lessons did he teach? Was he turning to the way of zealots?

When they finally reached Capernaum and sought out the house where Jesus taught, they could not get inside for the thickness of the crowd.

Aliza, thin as Passover bread, delivered word to someone inside, requesting that Jesus come see his family.

They waited for hours that day, and Jesus did not come.

Jude had thought his older brother crazy to disrespect them. To disrespect their mother.

Later that night, when they finally spoke to Jesus, his deep, soulful eyes penetrating and void of madness, he simply said, "I cannot come home. I must do my Father's work."

They walked home with wounded pride the following day. They wasted two days traveling and one extra day to wait for Jesus to come out of the house. Yes, it was good to see Jesus in his right mind, but that hardly made up for how far behind the woodshop would be once they returned home. It hardly made up for the fact that Jesus disgraced their family by insulting the teachers of the law.

Now, Jude allows a soft smile to form on his lips. Back then, he hadn't thought much further than his reputation—both keeping his family's name clean and keeping the family business in good order. He hadn't understood a lot of things about Jesus back then. He loved him, yes, but it wasn't until Jude spoke to him after his death—when the wounds still covered Jesus's hands—that it all began to make sense.

His brother, Jesus, the Son of Adonai, the Messiah.

Jude refocuses on the words before him. He'd entertained Jesus as a false teacher back then. Now, though, the Lord's church was in danger of true false teachers. Those who sought the prominence of their names over that of God. Jude himself knew this battle intimately. How many years had he introduced himself to fellow followers of the Way as "the Savior's brother"? As if growing up and living in the same household as Jesus gave him an eternal advantage?

Thankfully, Adonai pointed out the log in Jude's eye before he'd become too puffed up with himself.

He picks up his calamus and dips it in the inkwell.

Be merciful to those who doubt . . .

The Holy Spirit comes upon him, filling him with grace and gratitude until finally, he finishes his letter.

To the only God our Savior be glory, majesty, power, and authority, through Jesus Christ our Lord, before all ages, now and forevermore! Amen.

Reflection Questions

- We sometimes pride ourselves on the certainty we show regarding things of faith. What would it mean to "be merciful to those who doubt"?

  How does it change your perception of Bible characters to put yourself into the scene, imagining what it might have been like—the sounds, the smells, the conversations, the relationships?

Prayer

Father, help us lean deeper into you when things don't make sense to us. May we seek you and you alone this day. May we never put teachers of your Word above you, the Word. May we be merciful to those who don't believe the same as us. Lord, give us wisdom in these matters. Amen.

Suggested Reading

Mark 3:20–34
Book of Jude

FORTY

A New Mission

Inspired by Acts 9:1–31

His mission—his purpose—has never been clearer. It pushes him forward.

His pulse throbs. The heat of his breath meets the open air with force. It is zeal alone that strums the passion of Saul of Tarsus.

Shema Yisrael: Adhonai Elohenu, Adhonai Echad!

Hear, O Israel: the Lord our God, the Lord is one!

This is the story of his people. *Saul's* story. And he will do all in his power to step into his part. If only his people would stay true to HaShem instead of chasing after the ways of the nations around them.

Shema Yisrael: Adhonai Elohenu, Adhonai Echad!

He utters the prayer over and over, the meaning and power and history behind the words rooting within as he urges his donkey toward Damascus. He remembers the sealed letters, given to him by the high priest Caiaphas, in the leather cylinder at his belt. They will carry much weight in the Diaspora, where the Sanhedrin is highly respected.

A flash of Rabbi Gamaliel's face pokes through the depths of his prayers. Saul wishes they did not part how they did. He credits his teacher with his training as a young teen at the bet ha-midrash in Yerushalayim.

But Gamaliel did not approve of the stoning of that disciple of Jesus of Nazareth. He does not believe in taking such matters into the hands of men. Under normal circumstances, Saul does not condone violence, either.

But these are not normal circumstances.

These are desperate times—times that call forth the necessary zeal of the heroes of his faith. If he, both a Pharisee and a Roman citizen, cannot stand against harmful sects, who will?

On this, Saul leans toward the teachings of Shammai rather than the teachings of Gamaliel and Hillel. Those zealous for Adonai and his law must pray. They must sharpen their swords and ready themselves to fight.

Saul glances at the gray head of his donkey. He remembers the story of Balaam's donkey, of Phinehas's reward of an everlasting priestly covenant after he speared an unfaithful Israelite.

And what of Elijah, as he killed the worshipers of Baal? What of Judas Maccabee's zeal for the house of the Lord and the purity of his people? Were these not the stories of Israel? Saul's father recited them before prayers each morning as he helped Saul tie the tefillin to his arms and head.

Righteous heroes of their faith were lauded at every turn. Did HaShem not call Saul to a similar zeal in stomping out this ridiculous movement of Jesus of Nazareth's followers?

Of course he did. Saul would bring both men and women who followed the Way back to Yerushalayim in chains. He would wipe out this ridiculous crusade single-handedly, if he must.

Shema Yisrael: Adhonai Elohenu, Adhonai Echad!

A strange white light filters through the clouds ahead. A storm?

Paul slides off his donkey and stumbles toward the glow of pure light. Behind him, he hears the voices of his companions, but they sound like nonsense.

The light brightens. Is he having a vision as Ezekiel did?

A fracture splits the heavens, breaking them open as if Moses himself struck them with his staff. A figure stands above, dressed like a magnificent king in robes of shining authority.

Saul collapses to the ground, helpless to do anything but kneel, trembling before the skies.

"Saul! Saul! Why are you persecuting me?" The voice booms like thunder around him, loud and clear and magnanimous. An earthquake of declaration.

Saul blinks. The words do not make sense, even as he knows they are Adonai's. "Who are you, Lord?"

"I am Jesus, the one you are persecuting! Now get up and go into the city, and you will be told what you must do."

An explosion, instant and undeniable, shatters the innermost parts of Saul's being. It bursts apart everything he's ever known while at the same time piecing it all together. It splinters, but completes.

Saul struggles to his feet, groping for his donkey, but there is only darkness. The light has blinded him.

He has been blind.

His companions help him onto his donkey and guide the beast. They enter Damascus and search out their lodgings on Straight Street. His host, Judas, shows him his room, and Saul locks himself in, refusing food or drink.

He kneels on his pallet, praying. He welcomes the dark, soaking himself in it as he seeks answers.

Jesus of Nazareth is Adonai.

How had he not seen it before now? Jesus held heaven and earth together. Jesus was the fulfillment of all HaShem had promised. The Torah, the temple . . . they all pointed to *him*.

He had been so wrong.

He thinks of the disciple Stephen, perishing beneath a pile of rocks. What has he done?

Saul repents before the Almighty. He repents before Jesus.

He thinks of his parents and his sister, of his young sweetheart back in Tarsus. They will not understand, not right away. But he will make them. He will make everyone understand!

When a man named Ananias comes to him three days later, Saul is not surprised, for he saw him in a vision. Ananias lays trembling hands on Saul. "Brother Saul, the Lord Jesus, who appeared to you on the road, has sent me so that you might regain your sight and be filled with the Holy Spirit."

When Ananias lowers his hands, scales fall from Saul's eyes. He looks into the face of this man. His brother.

He has never seen so clearly. Grace and forgiveness and love and mercy sweep in, their anchor undeniable.

"Please, will you baptize me?" Saul wants nothing more than to die and rise with the Christ.

Ananias blinks. "You had come here to put us in chains."

"No longer. I see the error of my ways. Now, I see the risen King. I wish for nothing more than to share this good news with my people."

Saul is filled with zeal, but this time it is for a new mission. One that does not depend on chains and violence, but one that depends instead on grace and love and the power of a present hope fulfilled in the Son of God.

Jesus of Nazareth. Jesus, the Christ.

Reflection Questions

Jesus asks why Saul is persecuting him. What does this say about Jesus's relationship to his people? What does it say about how God might respond to your pain?

The stories Saul hears play a big part in forming him. How is this statement true for Saul after his conversion on the road to Damascus? What stories do you allow into your life?

Prayer

Father, thank you that nothing is impossible for you. You change our hearts, you renew our purpose, you give us a new vision and a new mission. Where we are blind to your love or to how we should act in your love, remove the scales from our eyes. May we move forward from the Lenten season without forgetting its holiness, without forgetting your holiness. Breathe life and hope into our hearts. Breathe Jesus into our spirits. Amen.

Suggested Reading

Acts 7–8:3

Acts 9:1–31

Acknowledgments

This book was an unexpected gift to write, and now that I am finally penning the acknowledgments, I'm realizing what a long list of people I have to thank for pouring into me and into this book!

When I first had the inkling to write a fictional book filled with secondary characters from the Gospels, I was both excited and cautious. I prayed and sought the wisdom of faith-filled people I respect. Thank you so much to Sarah Pudlo and Pastor Mike Pudlo for encouraging me to write these stories. Thank you to the ladies in my Bible study for praying me through some moments of deadline-approaching stress and especially to Tammy Rodrigues for being a true sister of my heart, for being innately curious when it comes to studying Scripture, and for never thinking my musings foolish.

Thank you to my agent, Cynthia Ruchti, for always championing me and my sometimes out-of-the-box ideas. A huge thanks to Rachel McRae not only for her initial interest in this book but for her valuable insight and feedback throughout the editing process. Thank you to Lauren Cole for help refining these stories and to Carrie Weston for her help getting them into the hands of readers! I'm so thankful for the entire team at Baker Publishing Group.

A big thank-you to my mother, Donna Anuszczyk, for her constant encouragement and support, as well as to my critique partner, Sandra Ardoin, for her help on this book.

I couldn't write a word without the unfailing support of my amazing husband, Daniel Chiavaroli, who not only builds me greenhouses and flowerbeds that keep me sane on the days when writing is hard but encourages me when life gets messy. I love you so much, honey!

Thank you to my sons, James and Noah, who have cheered me on since they were little boys. I can't believe you are both grown men—I'm so proud to be your mother.

Lastly, the greatest thank-you to the Author of Life. I like to think of my writing as an act of worship, but sometimes it's hard to see beyond the haze of deadlines and intense edits. Thank you for your immense grace in being with me in both the peace and the storms of writing and life. May this small piece of work glorify you, Jesus.

References

Bailey, Kenneth E. *Jesus Through Middle Eastern Eyes: Cultural Studies in the Gospels*. InterVarsity Press, 2008.

Beck, John A. *The Baker Illustrated Guide to Everyday Life in Bible Times*. Baker, 2013.

Brother Lawrence. *The Practice of the Presence of God*. Whitaker House, 1982.

Cobble, Tara-Leigh. *The Bible Recap*. Bethany House, 2020.

Comer, John Mark. *Practicing the Way*. Waterbrook, 2024.

Daniel-Rops, Henri. *Daily Life in the Times of Jesus*. Servant Books, 1962.

Edersheim, Alfred. *The Life and Times of Jesus the Messiah*. Hendrickson, 1993.

Grosvenor, Melville Bell, James B. Pritchard, A. Douglas Tushingham, et al. *Everyday Life in Bible Times*. National Geographic, 1967.

Guzik, David. *John: Verse by Verse Commentary*. Enduring Word, 2019.

Ignatius of Loyola. *The Spiritual Exercises of Saint Ignatius*. TAN Books, 1999.

Imes, Carmen Joy. *Being God's Image: Why Creation Still Matters*. InterVarsity Press, 2023.

Jethani, Skye. *The Divine Commodity: Discovering a Faith Beyond Consumer Christianity*. Zondervan, 2013.

Levine, Amy-Jill. *Entering the Passion: A Beginner's Guide to Holy Week*. Abingdon Press, 2018.

Levine, Amy-Jill. *The Gospel of Mark: A Beginner's Guide to the Good News*. Abingdon Press, 2023.

Levine, Amy-Jill. *Signs and Wonders: A Beginner's Guide to the Miracles of Jesus*. Abingdon Press, 2022.

McCaulley, Esau. *Lent: The Season of Repentance and Renewal*. InterVarsity Press, 2022.

New American Standard Bible. The Lockman Foundation, 1963.

Stern, David H. *The Complete Jewish Study Bible: Insights for Jews and Christians*. Hendrickson, 2016.

Wright, N. T. *Paul: A Biography*. HarperOne, 2020.

Heidi Chiavaroli is a hope-inspired storyteller writing from the deep curiosity of her own heart. Her debut novel, *Freedom's Ring,* was a Carol Award winner and a Christy Award finalist, a *Romantic Times* Top Pick, and a *Booklist* Top Ten Romance Debut. Her second Carol Award–winning novel, *The Orchard House*, is inspired by the lesser-known events in Louisa May Alcott's life and led her to write The Orchard House Bed and Breakfast series, a contemporary twist on *Little Women.* Lately, her stories have found her immersed deep in the world of the Bible, where she thinks she might like to stay for a while! Heidi makes her home in Massachusetts with her husband and two sons. Connect with her online at HeidiChiavaroli.com

Connect with Heidi:

HEIDICHIAVAROLI.COM

FACEBOOK @HeidiChiavaroli.Author

INSTAGRAM @HeidiChiavaroli

X (FORMERLY TWITTER) @HeidiChiavaroli

A Note from the Publisher

Dear Reader,

Thank you for selecting a Revell book! We're so happy to be part of your life through this work.

Revell's mission is to publish books that offer hope and help for meeting life's challenges, and that bring comfort and inspiration. We know that the right words at the right time can make all the difference; it is our goal with every title to provide just the words you need.

We believe in building lasting relationships with readers, and we'd love to get to know you better. If you have any feedback, questions, or just want to chat about your experience reading this book, please email us directly at publisher@revellbooks.com. Your insights are incredibly important to us, and it would be our pleasure to hear how we can better serve you.

We look forward to hearing from you and having the chance to enhance your experience with Revell Books.

The Publishing Team at Revell Books
A Division of Baker Publishing Group
publisher@revellbooks.com